Unresolved Identities

Unresolved Identities

*Discourse, Ambivalence,
and Urban Immigrant Students*

BIC NGO

Foreword by
Deborah P. Britzman

Published by
State University of New York Press, Albany

For information, contact State University of New York Press, Albany, NY
www.sunypress.edu

Production by Ryan Morris
Marketing by Anne M. Valentine

Library of Congress Cataloging-in-Publication Data

Ngo, Bic, 1974–
 Unresolved identities : discourse, ambivalence, and urban immigrant
students / Bic Ngo ; foreword by Deborah P. Britzman.
     p. cm. — (SUNY series, Second Thoughts: New Theoretical Formations)
 Includes bibliographical references and index.
 ISBN 978-1-4384-3057-7 (hardcover : alk. paper)
 ISBN 978-1-4384-3058-4 (pbk. : alk. paper)
  1. Immigrants—Education—United States. 2. Multicultural education—
United States. 3. Urban schools—United States. I. Title.

 LC3731.N65 2010
 371.826'9120973—dc22   2009023132

10 9 8 7 6 5 4 3 2 1

for my parents

Contents

Foreword

Readers are about to enter the ethnographic world of urban education. It is a contradictory world in that it receives, creates, and eludes an avalanche of ideas we have about the nature of education, adolescence and adulthood, culture, and research. However culturally dominant, no one idea can resolve this dynamic history. And we would do well to recognize, even in discourse, ironic signs. This present ethnography permits new ideas about urban culture and the participants who make and create it by proposing that while the ethnographer's act of writing seems to secure a reality to understand, in the act of reading culture with others, another reality is being written. In this novel education, we find urban education and ethnography as under construction. And this incompleteness gives us a renewed sense of what is slippery about experiencing and representing the excess of daily meaning: One story leads to another and the unexpected reply returns to open the story to the logic of the other and so, to new considerations of agency. Ethnography carries on this irony in its language: As one word leads to another, as signifiers, then, are lost and found, identities are figured, created, and affected. Readers then encounter traces of identity through the poetics of ambivalence. Each story of identity, itself an emotional situation, signifies a world of love and hate, desire and compliance, and important questions.

Ethnography bears a promise of second thoughts, or critical commentary on its own processive meaning. In reading these stories of urban education we can begin to wonder why the experience of education feels so timeless and repetitive. Bic Ngo instructs readers to move beyond the romance of the ethnographic present as well and to become surprised by the ways the writing of ethnography itself becomes a character in this play. Our author invites us to critique static views as stories of constraint and imposition, indeed as discourse. She presents, with great sensitivity, the idea that participants who live the dissonant history of urban education are also those who question it. In this ethnography, language becomes our fight for certainty, our wish to represent what is most uncertain about us, and our fragile ties to others. Ethnography plays in the field of speech and our ethnographer, Bic Ngo, knows this well.

So readers meet what is most peculiar about reading and writing culture. These literary acts are the procedures for becoming somebody, but they are also the activities that cohere in school topics and sometimes become caught in or confused by school authority and resistance to it. Here, we have one corner of what is now thought of as "the crisis of representation." Ngo's ethnography begins in this dilemma, whereby the problem of writing culture is not only that representation configures partiality and contradiction. This study proposes that with the linguistic turn, with the understanding that reality is always interpretive reality and therefore subjectively constructed, something happens to both reality and ethnography. Once subjective dynamics of ambivalence, doubt, fantasy, and desire are taken as forms of agency; reality itself becomes dynamic reality and we can think about why interpretation matters to learning to live. Another way of putting this is that ethnography is affected by ineffable subjective events and in this sense gives testimony to the crisis of representation.

As for the ethnographer, she, too, is both a part of this dynamic reality and an invention of it. In more than a few research stories, and in her dialogue with youth, the ethnographer finds herself joined in the adolescent situation: the writing tries on identities accoutrements, fights with old meanings, secures and bothers the advent of belief, and gestures toward what is most anxious and pleasurable about the work of becoming a subject. The story searches for itself and along the way, readers, too, may become caught up in dynamic culture. Bic Ngo presents readers with the ironic situation that even as the ethnographer admits the problem of interpretation, the enterprise of ethnography is wildly intersubjective. This means, among other things, that writing culture is the work of second thoughts and proposing the interpretive dilemma as to how it comes to be that these second thoughts are so difficult to think.

Bic Ngo narrates how she herself has changed because of "hanging out" with Lao American adolescents in a place she names, with great irony, "Dynamic High." Even the term "hanging out" signifies dynamic emotional situations of being with others. The youth are the teachers here, but as any teacher knows, the student ethnographer must disappoint before she, too, can be approached as a complex, motivated

subject. In this intersubjective space, meanings signify the sighs of contradictions and the demands for hope. Dynamic High is on the move,
even if adults who work there can barely keep up, defend against their
irrelevancy, and take too long to get the youth's messages. And it is difficult to keep up with these youth since, like the adults who surround
them, their communicative emotional world runs from the ridiculous
to the sublime. Adults are failing their tests since the youth themselves
must create a world adults barely remember or need to forget. How it
comes to be that a place called Dynamic High is sometimes caught in
the fixations of urban education's imaginary is part of this story and its
analysis proposes that urban education signifies more than the demise
of the city, the clash of cultures and generations, and the immigrant's
dreams and anxieties. There are also libidinal ties between youth and
community, and then urban education becomes a transitional space
between newly chosen and the barely inherited. These are scenes of
love and hate, belonging and alienation, sexuality and aggression, jeal-
ously and guilt, and so, a world of ambivalence. Second thoughts may
help us understand that what is most dynamic about Dynamic High are
the youth themselves. They are always constructing that great cultural
construction known as identity, itself a desire for recognition.

The other irony that Bic Ngo's ethnography gives to us readers
comes from her repeated question to youth and to teachers after they
explain some emotional situation, some worry, or some breakdown in
meaning. Ngo asks them, "What do you mean?" The question itself
is a mini ethnography of language. More words are made, suggesting
that stories are portals to more meaning, or a temporary stop on the
way to encountering what is most unruly, uncertain, and abundant
within dynamic intersubjectivity. Nothing stays the same: Even the stories seem to lag behind the experience and so ask us to think more
deeply about what is excessive in schooling, in identity, in culture, and
in existence as such. If the cliché has an afterlife in education and
has, at times, achieved mythic status in research itself, Ngo reminds
readers that these events also create the greatest challenge for educators and researchers. They, too, can question received knowledge and
analyze their own passion for ignorance. We can begin to think about
the complicated, fleeting world of youth and their identity migrations,
not as so many problems to be resolved but as forms of life—new
communications to learn.

Bic Ngo's ethnography contributes to the SUNY book series called
Second Thoughts: New Theoretical Formations. It joins other ethnographies,
theoretical works, and philosophical studies on the problem of thinking

education differently. I began this series in 2002, and it now draws to a close. With each book, however, readers are invited into the surprise of second thoughts with new approaches to old conflicts in a field called education.

Deborah P. Britzman

Acknowledgments

For the past several years I have sought to better understand the experiences of urban, immigrant students and families. This book is one of the products of this work. It builds on work from my dissertation, conference presentations, and previous iterations that have appeared in *Equity and Excellence in Education, International Journal of Qualitative Studies in Education,* and *Theory into Practice.* My work has been enriched by comments and conversations from numerous individuals, including reviewers, editors, mentors, colleagues, students, and friends.

I owe much to Stacey Lee, Amy Stambach, Gloria Ladson-Billings, Michael Apple, Carl Grant and other mentors from the University of Wisconsin–Madison. They nurtured my thinking about teaching and learning in ways that underscore the complexities of life. Their dedication to issues of equity and diversity significantly informed my own resolve to work toward social justice. I am fortunate to do much of this work with colleagues with similar commitments, who provide me with warmth, kindness, and inspiration. Special thanks to Martha Bigelow, Kevin Kumashiro, Cynthia Lewis, Jill Leet-Otley and Anne Zoellner for offering critical feedback to drafts of this book. Tim Lensmire, Misty Sato, Thom Swiss, Kendall King, and J. B. Mayo all feed my soul and mind in remarkable ways. I am grateful to have such brilliant colleagues whom I can also call friends.

This book would not be possible without the Dynamic High students, teachers, and staff, who allowed me into their lives and community. I am obliged to them for letting me share their experiences. But more than this, by opening their world to me, they revealed insights into my own life. For this book, I am also indebted to Deborah Britzman and Jane Bunker for their editorial guidance and generous support. The inclusion of my work in the Second Thoughts Series is a tremendous honor for me. For all of these things, I am deeply thankful.

Outside of the academy, friends such as Stephanie Schlichting, Craig Schlichting, Pam Sukhum, Pat Sukhum, John Castillo, Keith Bias, Jeff Bauer, Todd Wilkinson, Molly Gordon, Stacy Johnson, Gretchen Bias, Heidi Gastler, and Cathy Grady bring richness to my world. They sustain me with much laughter, silliness, and love. They worry over me, give me hugs, and refuse to let my work dominate my life. They are family.

I do not have adequate words to express my gratitude and love for my parents and siblings. Tommy, Kim, Diem, and Phi keep me grounded and comforted in a way that recalls and renews our shared family history. My mom and dad are in a league of their own. Their patience, intelligence, and courage become more apparent with each passing year. I am humbled by the goodness of their humanity and the expanse of their love for me.

1

Introduction

> I am in the paradoxical position of deploying what is conventionally
> known as an antihumanist discourse for humanist means. That is,
> my emphasis on complexity, power, contradiction, discursive produc-
> tion and ambiguity is invoked in part to demonstrate complexity
> and irony in the lives of the people I knew, in order to complicate
> and dismantle the ready stereotypes that erase complexity in favor
> of simple, unitary images.
>
> —Dorinne K. Kondo, *Crafting Selves*

It is passing time at Dynamic High School.[1] Along with approximately
1,500 students, I am trying to navigate my way through the school to
the next class without jostling too many people or running into the
heels of the students in front of me. Amidst the din of students greeting each other and trying to have conversations by shouting over their
peers, I am quietly thinking about the end of my year-long research
at the school. With only a few weeks left before the end of the school
year, I am anticipating missing the students who have been a part of
my daily life for 9 months. I think about the Lao American students
whom I have followed closely. I think about their Hmong American,
African American, White American, and Liberian American peers and
friends. As I recall the stories that they shared and the inside school
and outside school activities that I witnessed, I think about the ways
dominant understandings of urban education confine and constrain
their identities as students and human beings. I think about the adolescent girls with children who are understood pejoratively as "single
mothers." I think about the adolescent boys struggling to belong, who
are understood simplistically as "gangsters."

This book grows out of a compelling need to understand and
explicate the complexities of the experiences of urban, immigrant
students. In my work at Dynamic High School, I discovered that in
many ways the experiences and identities of the students I came to

know reproduced the familiar representations of urban and immigrant students. However, and significantly, I also found that dominant understandings of urban education failed to account for the incongruities and complexities of the identities and lives of students. In large part, this is due to the framing of urban residents and immigrant identities within restrictive, binary oppositions.

Background

Discourses About Urban Identities

Popular images about urban life depict a depressing picture of urban schools and communities. They portray youth idling on street corners and communities scarred by graffiti and litter, with buildings and homes in disrepair. Informed by research on the inner-city family (Moynihan, 1965), the culture of poverty (Lewis, 1969), and the urban underclass (Wilson, 1987), these prevailing ideas about urban communities and residents are marked by a language of social pathology. Urban communities and residents are described as "welfare-dependent," "crime-ridden," and "violence-prone." Likewise, the dominant ideas about urban students and schools include "run-down," "gang-ruled," "failing," and "not meeting standards." Ironically, these deficit discourses come from research that attempted to illustrate the challenges faced by urban students and families. Opponents of this research have criticized the implicit message that the social and economic problems faced by urban residents are directly and causally linked to their cultural values and characteristics (Haymes, 1995). Despite such criticism, the widely circulated negative narratives continue to define urban communities, schools, and students as failing and dysfunctional. The residents of the "ghettos" are positioned as responsible for their own social and economic situation.

A second widespread understanding of urban schools and communities is informed by the response from educational researchers to this early deficit-centered research. Rather than holding urban families culpable, education researchers attempted to elucidate the impact of social inequalities (Kozol, 1991); school reform (McNeil, 2000); in-school sorting (Oakes, 1985); racism (Lee, 2005); and subtractive schooling (Valenzuela, 1999) on the reproduction of social inequality and school under-achievement. Other researchers sought to highlight the successes of urban schools and residents. Ladson-Billings (1994), for example, illustrated the success of "culturally relevant" teachers and practices in the achievement of African American students. Similarly, others underscored the ways urban teachers and students are able to overcome challenges and obstacles to achieve success (Corwin, 2000; Michie, 1999).

Today, the influence of this work is reflected in two dominant discourses about urban education. On one hand, there is a tendency to emphasize dysfunction and failure; and on the other hand, there is a tendency to emphasize resilience and success. Media stories abound that highlight poor test scores, gangs, drugs, poverty, and violence in depictions of urban schools. These dominant representations point to the presence of poverty, substance abuse, crime, unemployment, early pregnancy, and gang involvement as contributing to the increase of urban social problems in general and the failure of urban education in particular. At the same time, images and rhetoric about urban triumph also dominate the popular imagination. Popular films such as *Dangerous Minds* (1995), *Stand and Deliver* (1988), and *Freedom Writers* (2007) ubiquitously spotlight the dedication of teachers and the perseverance of students that allow them to "beat the odds" and achieve success. While these films reiterate and reify urban problems, they also exemplify the penchant to underscore urban "success stories." On the whole, these dominant discourses have created an understanding of urban education and experiences that are characterized by binary frameworks of success/failure and functional/dysfunctional.

Discourses About Immigrant Identities

In much the same way, pervasive notions of immigrant students and families frame their experiences and identities within dualistic categories. We can see this in the numerous media accounts of the resettlement and socialization experiences of recent immigrants to the United States. The storylines are familiar, as they echo decades of news reports by emphasizing a binary division of differences between immigrant cultures and U.S. culture. As the stories usually go, immigrant families are contending with a "clash" of cultures, and immigrant youth are caught or torn "between two cultures." Ubiquitous headlines inscribe the quandary: "Generation 1.5: Young immigrants in two worlds" (Feagans, 2006), "Taking on two worlds" (Do, 2002), and "Mother's fray: Culture clash puts special strain on immigrant moms and daughters" (Wax, 1998).

In a story about two Lao immigrant students, for example, academic achievements were celebrated as the accomplishments of immigrants who "have worked past roadblocks to grow into strong students and 'great people' who are both bilingual and bicultural" (Denn, 2000,

p. B1). According to this story of bicultural success, the students were able to demonstrate the mastery of the "traditional" and "modern" aspects of their identities through the ability to perform "a traditional Laotian dance 'beautifully, gracefully' one day and then . . . hip-hop dances the next" (p. B1). In a different tone, another story (Taylor, 1998) about Somali immigrants in the United States explained how Somali families were "working through the clash of cultures." According to this narrative on the adaptation of Somali immigrants, while "drugs don't appear to be a major problem among Somalis," domestic violence is prevalent because "[s]ome men may be reacting violently if their wives don't adhere to traditional ways" (p. 1A). In the collision between U.S. and Somali cultures, the adherence of Somali men to "tradition" gives rise to acts of domestic violence.

Similarly, a special series about Hmong youth bemoaned the fact that Hmong girls who have been raped by Hmong gang members have been "shamed into silence" (Louwagie & Browning, 2005a, 2005b) by Hmong culture and so do not report their experiences of sexual abuse. Pitting notions of Hmong cultural beliefs against those of U.S. society, the story explained the "shame" of one Hmong girl:

> By losing her virginity without marriage—even violently, against her will—she had violated a basic tenet of her Hmong culture. If her family found out, they would feel forever shamed. She feared her culture would require her to marry one of her attackers to save her reputation (Louwagie & Browning, 2005a, p. 1A).

As Louwagie and Browning (2005b) allege, "culture clash can stymie help" (p. 11A) for Hmong girls who have been raped by Hmong gang members. In their explication of the culture clash, the journalists underscore the role of cultural difference:

> Adapting any non-Western culture to the United States is a formidable task. For the Hmong community, which hails from isolated mountain villages in Laos and refugee camps in Thailand, settling in urban areas such as St. Paul has meant a bigger change (Louwagie & Browning 2005b, p. 11A).

Here, the identity and culture—beliefs, behaviors, and values—of immigrants such as the Hmong are characterized as traditional and rural, in contrast to a highly modern and civilized U.S. society. Of particular concern are the differences between the first-generation (parents) and second-generation (youth) that create a clash between the "traditional" values of immigrant parents versus "modern" values of youth who are influenced by contemporary U.S. practices:

> The problem comes in mixing Hmong traditions with American culture, many agree. While Hmong refugees are struggling to survive in a culture foreign to them, their children are adapting more quickly and disobeying what they see as their parents' antiquated rules (Louwagie & Browning 2005b, p. 11A).

Implicitly and explicitly, the values and practices of Hmong immigrant parents are depicted as "antiquated"—backward or stuck in time. In contrast, immigrant children are positioned as "adapting more quickly." The assertion that the "problem comes in mixing Hmong traditions with American culture" constructs the cultures of different ethnic and national groups as irreconcilably distinct. Hmong and American cultures are both positioned as naturalized and static, impervious to influence and change.

Narratives about immigrant experiences that underscore biculturalism, a "clash of cultures," "traditional ways," or some sort of "basic tenet" of culture are by and large attempts to illustrate the *changes* in the lives of immigrant students and families. Instead, and problematically, they position immigrants within dualistic categories of modern/traditional or First World/Third World. As a consequence, immigrant groups are portrayed as developmentally and socially backward or suspended in time. In a similar vein, accounts about urban residents that point to the challenges of poverty and triumph over gangs, violence, and inequality are attempts to demonstrate the complex dimensions of urban life and human experiences. However, they result in either/or characterizations of urban students and families as good/bad, hardworking/lazy or functional/dysfunctional.

The experiences of the urban, immigrant students I knew from Dynamic High were messier and more contradictory than these smooth, easy storylines that have dominated our imagination. Missing from these simplistic accounts of urban, immigrant experiences are the background and context that point to unfinished, precarious identities and contested social relations. This book is an attempt to unmask and examine the stories that we tell about urban, immigrant students. It is also an attempt to highlight and work through the contradictions of identity and to unsettle the hegemony of discourses that frame identities within discrete, binary categories.

Theorizing Immigrant Identity

Criticism of the notion of identity and cultures as unitary, immutable, isolable entities is not new. For the past several decades, social and cultural theorists have pointed to the existence of multiple, intersecting, and competing identities as well as the ways in which cultures and identities are essentialized (e.g., Du Bois, 1953; Anzaldua, 1987; Hall, 1990; Bhabha, 1994; Lowe, 1996). Anzaldua's (1987) work, for example, has played a critical role in revealing the experiences of living on the "border" between two cultures, and the ways border identities are fractured by race, class, gender, and sexuality. Writing about the Asian American immigrant experience in the United States, Lowe (1996) elaborates on the difficulty of using an "Asian American identity" as an organizing and political tool because of the tendency to fix culture and identity. Instead, Lowe argues for an understanding of Asian American identity as socially constructed and situationally specific, emphasizing its "heterogeneity, hybridity and multiplicity" (p. 60).

A major problem with viewing cultures and identities as coherent wholes is that it overlooks critical inequalities, contradictions, and differences. As Ladson-Billings (2000) points out, "each [ethnic] group is constituted of myriad national and ancestral origins, but the dominant ideology of the Euro-American epistemology has forced each into an essentialized and totalized unit that is perceived to have little or no internal variation" (p. 260). The totalization of Asian American identities, for example, lumps fifth-generation Chinese Americans with first-generation Lao immigrants in the same Asian American success story. Advocating the need to uncover the "complexities of difference," Ladson-Billings (2000) pressed educational researchers to "work in racialized discourses and ethnic epistemologies" (p. 271).

Despite the continual denial of culture and identity as discrete, immutable wholes, we still struggle to speak and teach about culture in ways that affirm its fluidity. In various contexts, the "culture" of different groups is still conceptualized discursively and pedagogically as some "thing" that is naturally occurring and fixed in time. The academic achievement of students of color, for example, is often explained by culture-based arguments that underscore ideas about discrete, unitary cultures of different racial and ethnic groups. These arguments contend that African American boys do not do well in school due to a "cult of anti-intellectualism" (McWhorter, 2000); while Asian American students achieve academic success because of "traditional" family values and a strong work ethic (Caplan, Choy, & Whitmore, 1991; Zhou & Bankston, 1998).

For immigrant students, a hallmark of the efforts to make sense of their particular experiences is revealed in the discourse of students being torn "between two worlds." As we saw in the news stories above, the struggles of immigrant students with peers, parents, and U.S. society are understood to arise from the tensions between disparate cultural norms and expectations. One dimension of this bimodal framework sets up a dichotomy of immigrant culture versus U.S. culture. The decisions of immigrant students to drop out of school to marry, for example, are viewed as choices that align with values that are different from those of dominant U.S. society. The identity and cultures of immigrants and that of mainstream society are viewed to be in conflict. Another dimension of the "between two worlds" discourse creates a first-generation (parents) versus second-generation (youth) dichotomy that manifests in a preoccupation with "intergenerational conflict." Disputes that immigrant youth and adults have over clothes or dating restrictions are construed to be conflicts between the values of immigrant parents that are still tied to "traditional" beliefs and those of immigrant youth who are influenced by contemporary U.S. practices.

While I want to recognize that this research on cultural conflict has been essential to advancing our understanding of the challenges faced by immigrant students and families, I also want to talk back to and extend this literature. Problematically, as Lowe (1996) persuasively argues, "the reduction of the cultural politics of racialized ethnic groups, like Asian Americans, to first-generation/second-generation struggles displaces social differences into a privatized familial opposition" (p. 63). This focus on the "generation gap" deflects attention from the politics of exclusion and differentiation that are experienced by immigrants. Further, explanations of immigrant experiences and identities as connected to "traditional" cultural values set up binary oppositions between traditional and modern, East and West, and First World and Third World. Culture and identity are reified into immutable, unitary entities at the same time that they are inscribed with priority and hierarchy (i.e., good/bad, ours/theirs). Ultimately, the experiences of immigrant youth are represented as if they are seamless, without contradictions and change.

Within the research on the identities of immigrant students, a small body of literature has been important for advancing knowledge on the multiplicity of student identities. For example, Lee (1996) challenged the monolithic identity of Asian American students as a "model minority" by demonstrating the variation in experience and achievement of students from different Asian ethnic groups. More recently, Lee (2001) argued that Hmong American students are more than model minorities or delinquents, by pointing to the ways structural forces and relationships inside and outside schools shape their attitudes toward and experiences in school. In their classic piece, McKay and Wong (1996) illuminated the multiple and shifting identities of adolescent immigrant Chinese students as they are shaped by and react to discourses about achievement and language learning.

Especially pioneering research specifically rejected the idea that immigrant students are either simply internalizing the dictates of their families and communities or those of mainstream society and emphasized instead the ways the identities of immigrant youth are fragmented, and how they change across different social contexts. British-Sikh immigrant students in Hall's (1995) study viewed themselves as neither entirely English nor entirely Indian. Hall put forth the notion of "cultural fields" to stress the situational aspect of identities, highlighting identity as positional and subject to change. The cultural fields that make up the lives of British-Sikh adolescents are composed "of constellations of power and authority, cultural competencies and influences" (p. 253) specific to each cultural field. As Hall (1995) further elaborates, the

> practices in a cultural field both reproduce and create cultural expectations for bodily gestures and dress, for appropriate manners and signs of respect between the generations and the sexes, as well as the cultural knowledge people use to interpret social interactions (p. 253).

According to Hall, the shifts in the practices and relations of power from one social context to the next allow second-generation British-Sikh youth to "play" with cultural identities. In each cultural field, such as school, home, shopping mall, or temple, the adolescents participate in and create different cultural forms. As a result, British-Sikh youth construct "not one unitary cultural identity, but rather multiple cultural identities that acquire situationally specific meanings and forms" (Hall, 1995, p. 253).

Similarly, Sarroub (2005) found that Yemeni adolescents adapted their identities to the cultural spaces they inhabited. These adolescents strategically used Arabic in school for "important functional and religious purposes as students attempted to maintain dual identities" (p. 61). Likewise, the Indian American students in Maira's (2002) study switched among multiple identities as they moved between the spaces of school, work, and family, changing from baggy pants and earrings they wore with peers to more conservative attire for work and family gatherings. According to Maira, Indian American youth are creating a "cut 'n mix" style that is neither like the music, fashion, and practices of their parents nor that of dominant U.S. society.

Taken together, this growing body of literature on immigrant students highlights the identities of immigrant youth as those that respond to ideological, cultural, and structural forces in schools and society. Importantly, it points to the various discourses and practices that inform and shape the experiences and identities of students in ways that are multiple and shifting. However, this literature on the multiplicity and fluidity of immigrant identity has primarily focused on identity shifting across various *social contexts*. My research with the urban, immigrant students at Dynamic High School suggests that immigrant identities are much messier and conflictual than notions of "multiple," "situational" or "fluid" identities. Moreover, and importantly, my work illuminates the ambivalence—contradictions, uncertainty, fractures—of *individual* identities, where the subject position of a person shifts with each speaking, from one moment to the next. From this perspective, identities are not just "multiple," "hybrid," and "situated," but significantly, they are also subdivided, inconsistent, and temporary.[2]

Discourse, Identity, and Ambivalence

In this study, I draw on the work of poststructural and postcolonial theorists to understand the experiences and identities of urban, immigrant students through the conceptual lens of ambivalence. I use *discourse* to refer to spoken and written language as well as images used in popular and academic arenas. As a network of power relations and knowledges, discourses are more than simply a group of statements or images. Weedon (1987) lucidly explains this Foucauldian definition of discourse:

> Discourses, in Foucault's work, are ways of constituting knowledge, together with the social practices, forms of subjectivity and power relations which inhere in such knowledges and the relations between them. Discourses are more than ways of thinking and producing meaning. They constitute the "nature" of the body, unconscious and conscious mind and emotional life of the subjects they seek to govern. Neither the body nor thoughts and feelings have meaning outside their discursive articulation, but the ways in which discourse constitutes the minds and bodies of individuals is always part of a wider network of power relations, often with institutional bases (p. 108).

More than language or ways to understand our world, discourses are a set of historically grounded, yet dynamic statements and images that have the power to legitimate and create knowledges, identities, and realities. The power of discourses to constitute the identities of Asian Americans through the discourse of the model minority is illustrative. According to the discourse of the Asian American model minority, the achievements of Asian Americans are attributable to cultural values, familial support, and a strong work ethic (Lee, 1996; Osajima, 1987). It emerged in the 1960s in the midst of the Civil Rights movement and was often used to contrast the experiences of successful Asian American "minorities" against "troublemaking" ones (e.g., African Americans and Latino Americans) (Osajima, 1987). The discourse of the model minority positions and legitimates Asian Americans as "successful" minorities, while simultaneously blaming other racial groups for their underachievement. As this example illustrates, discourses are never neutral but are imbued with and reflect political positions, values, and social practices (Hall, 1990; Weedon, 1987).

An important assumption of my understanding of discourse is that some discourses have become so ingrained through repeated circulation that they have become institutionalized and reproduced in social, cultural, and political processes (e.g., law, education, medicine, social welfare) (Davies, 2000; Weedon, 1987). These dominant discourses are so frequently employed in our social and discursive practices that they seem to be "natural" or self-evident. The naturalization of dominant discourses masks their *social construction* and conceals the existence of competing, alternative discourses (Mills, 1997; Weedon, 1987). For instance, the dominant discourse of Asian American success prescribes and defines the experiences of a "normal" Asian American as obedient, quiet, passive, and academically successful (Lee, 1996). These discursive frameworks define the parameters within which Asian ethnics can negotiate what it means to be Asian American. Because dominant discourses have the power to confine and control what it means to be Asian American, behaviors of Asian American women and men that fall outside the discourse of the model minority are understood to be unnatural and deviant. Hegemonic discourses obscure competing accounts of academic struggle, social marginalization, and other possibilities and realities of being Asian American.

When considering *identity*, I understand it as a dynamic process of "production" that is constructed, negotiated and constituted through discourse and representation (Hall, 1990, 1996; Davies, 1993; Weedon, 1987). As Hall (1996) explains,

precisely because identities are constructed within, not outside discourse, we need to understand them as produced
in specific historical and institutional sites within specific
discursive formations and practices, by specific enunciative
strategies. Moreover, they emerge within the play of specific
modalities of power, and thus are more the product of the
marking of difference and exclusion, than they are the sign
of an identical, naturally-constituted unity (p. 4).

Instead of naturally given, identity is produced through discursive
practices that take place within specific historical and social contexts
and power relations. Because identity is constructed through the play
of power and exclusion within social and discursive practices, identity is a discursive *positioning* that is unstable, incomplete, and always
changing (Hall, 1990, 1996). From this perspective, characterizations
of immigrants as traditional, patriarchal, and resistant to assimilation-
ist demands are not simply natural, harmless representations. Instead,
they reflect the dynamics of power relations and are the product of
repeated expression and circulation in public and academic discourse.
For example, discourses about Asian Americans as the "yellow peril"
and "model minority" have historical roots in U.S. labor and civil rights
movements, respectively (Lee, 1999). Likewise, the ever-present discourse
that immigrants are a burden on the U.S. economy is grounded in
social welfare standpoints and political motivations.

　　　Identity invokes a history of ideas and images—discourses—of who
we are (Bhabha, 1994; Davies, 1993, 2000; Hall, 1996) as a point of
"temporary attachment to the subject positions which discursive practices construct for us" (Hall, 1996, p. 6). From this point of "temporary
attachment" we depart and respond—in our identity constructions—to
practices, discourses, and representations that have already identified
us (Davies, 1993). The ways we respond may echo, contradict, modify,
or resist how we have been represented. Identity thus involves a double
action, where in one movement we are *put* in subject positions by others who draw on available, powerful discourses to identify us; and in
another movement we *take up* subject positions by drawing on available discourses ourselves. In other words, identity can be constituted
in two ways. First, one can position or identify another individual by
adopting a discourse that draws on a particular cultural stereotype
(e.g., as an Asian American model minority) to identify the person as
a particular kind of subject (e.g., as high-achieving). And second, one
can position oneself by taking up storylines to locate oneself within

a specific identity. For instance, Asian American students may choose
to identify themselves as anti-school. In both cases, positioning is not
necessarily intentional (Davies, 2000). Moreover, due to the existence
of multiple discourses that say numerous, even contradictory things
about who individuals are or can be, the identities or positioning of
individuals are continuously constituted and susceptible to disagreement and inconsistency.

In this book I examine this double movement of identity, specifically how Lao students work with—rework—discourses that have already
identified them. According to Bhabha (1994), the meaning of identity
and culture is not tied down permanently, but forever bears the traces
of other meanings. Because meaning has no fixity, it opens up a space
for ambivalence and re-articulation. Bhabha (1994) maintains that "we
should remember that it is the 'inter'—the cutting edge of translation
and negotiation, the in-between space—that carries the burden of the
meaning of culture" (p. 38). This space of translation or identification enables other identities to emerge by constituting the discursive
conditions where "the same signs [discourses, representations] can be
appropriated, translated, rehistoricized and read anew" (Bhabha, 1994,
p. 37). Identities that are shaped in and come out of this space of
translation are therefore new, "neither One nor the Other but *something
else besides, in-between*" (Bhabha, 1994, p. 219). As I make sense of the
experiences and identities of the students (and teachers) at Dynamic
High School, I pay particular attention to the ways that discourses and
representations are (and need to be) read anew.

To emphasize that identity and identity work are "fragmented and
fractured; never singular but multiply constructed across different, often
intersecting and antagonistic, discourses, practices and positions" (Hall,
1996, p. 4), I specifically employ the notion of *ambivalence* to describe
and make sense of the identities of Lao immigrant students. Cultural
theorists such as Bhabha (1994) have theorized culture and identity
through interchangeable terms of "ambivalent space," "hybridity," "third
space," "in-between," "liminality," "meanwhile," and "supplementary."
In the following pages, I give preference to the term *ambivalence* to
underscore that the space of identity work is not a fixed location,
with originary ideas of identity and culture as pure, discrete points of
departure (Bhabha 1990). *Ambivalence* is able to signal the continual
fluctuations, contradictions, incompleteness, and uncertainty of identity
work that, for me, terms such as "hybridity" and "in-between" do not
capture as well. For example, "in-between" suggests that the identities
of Lao students are perhaps *between* Asian and U.S. cultures. Problem-

atically, it recasts dualisms that my work seeks to unsettle. The term *ambivalence* is better able to disrupt the framing of urban, immigrant identities within binary oppositions. It is better able to emphasize the multiple, fragmented, and inconsistent identities that urban, Lao American students create as they draw on a range of (competing) discourses in their meaning-making.

Collecting and Telling Stories

"Hanging Out" Research

> *Lori, Nikhong, Coua, Somkiat, and I are all sitting at the booth today. We are crowded together, with Lori and Somkiat sitting on one side of the booth, and Coua and me on the other side. Nikhong is sitting in a chair that she has pulled up to the end of the booth. We're discussing what we did during "Issues Day" yesterday. There's a consensus among the students that the day was boring in general, but good because the regular classes were cancelled. As we begin to talk about the different workshops the students attended, Somkiat loudly complains that he got classes that he didn't want because he didn't sign up for any of them. And to make matters worse, he was also late to school. After a brief moment where Coua, Lori, Nikhong, and I glance at each other with suppressed grins, Coua says, "Well, duh!" We tease Somkiat a little more, and then he tells us that he went to workshops such as HIV and safe sex, which were just "okay." Lori shares that she went to one on rape and dating violence, but didn't like it at all. She thought that it would focus more on protection and prevention, but instead, the focus was on what to do after the assault. Nikhong then gushes about how much she loved her Fun with Chemistry class, mainly because they got to make ice cream. More quietly, she also mentions that Vong was in the class with her, but she didn't talk to him. When I ask why, Nikhong blushes and reminds me that she's still too embarrassed that he knows that she wanted to ask him to the Sadie Hawkins dance. As I lean toward Nikhong to tell her that it is really brave to ask someone out, I accidentally knock over Somkiat's Coke. Coua leaves us to get napkins to help me clean up the spill. As he walks away, Phongsava runs over to our booth and plops down next to me, where Coua was sitting moments before. She immediately takes out a bunch of pictures that she had taken with Somkiat and Lori.*

Lori picks out a picture of her and Somkiat to keep and Somkiat takes a picture of him and Phongsava. As we talk about the pictures, I learn that Phongsava used to date one of Lori's older brothers. While we pour over the pictures, Coua comes back with the napkins and hands them to me and leaves again to sit with some of his Hmong friends.

Suddenly, in her usual frenetic manner, Phongsava turns to me and tells me that she's leaving Dynamic to go to an alternative school. Ms. Jefferson referred her to the school because she doesn't have enough credits to pass the year. As Phongsava tells me she's supposed to leave as soon as possible, I think back to the numerous days she skipped school and the attempts by me and Ms. Sanders to encourage her to come to school more. Phongsava tells us that she doesn't want to go, but that she has to because of her grades. Sensing our concern, she assures us that she'll try to come back to Dynamic next year. Somkiat then breaks in with his own news, sharing that he and his mom are moving to one of the southern suburbs in June. Even though it will be almost an hour from his dad, siblings, and friends, Somkiat announces that it will be good, since they'll be living "in a kind of circle" near three other aunts. Lori and I point out it will be different living so far from the city and Somkiat declares, "I'm going to be white-washed!" When I ask him to explain, he tells me that the city will have mainly White people, and that his family will be the only minorities. . . . With a few minutes left in the lunch period, Somkiat asks me where I'm going next. I tell him that I'm going to Civics with Lori and Nikhong. He makes a disapproving noise of "Mmm" and then asks, "Why don't you go to class with me?" More than words, his tone conveys that he thinks it'd be much better than going with Lori and Nikhong. I glance at Lori and Nikhong, and tell Somkiat that I already made plans with the girls to go to class with them. In an attempt to lessen his disappointment, I suggest that I could go to class with him tomorrow or anytime after today. Still unhappy with me, Somkiat gives me a disapproving look, makes another "Mmm" and then grudgingly agrees (FN 3/6/02, 2nd Lunch).

The process of doing ethnography is one of learning about the lives of others, your discipline, and ultimately, yourself (Glesne, 2005). Perhaps more than anything, ethnography is an engagement of social relations that muddles who we think we are as "researchers."

Over the course of the 2001–2002 academic year I spent an extensive amount of time with Lao students inside and outside Dynamic High School.[3] In school, I followed the students through various activities that included attending class, lunch, and school-sponsored dances and sports games. Outside school, I was invited to spend time with students at family gatherings, church, restaurants, parks, or in their homes. This "hanging out" research, as a friend called it, involved engaging with students on a personal level as individuals, and not simply as research participants or "informants." Indeed, as a refugee of the Vietnam War who came to the United States as a young girl, my life experiences were very similar to those of my participants. My interactions with the Lao American students challenged insider/outsider notions of researcher identities.[4] Rather than positioning myself as a "fly on the wall," in my work at Dynamic, doing ethnography was about immersing myself in the day-to-day experiences of students, and opening myself up to the activities, interests, worries, and emotions of their lives. As the above fieldnote illustrates, the ethnographic experience of "being there" includes being present for the unfolding of Nikhong's crush on a boy, for the sharing of news about Phongsava's move to an alternative school, and for the routine of having lunch with students. My presence during this particular lunch hour, where Somkiat shared that he went to a workshop on safe sex and HIV during *Issues Day*,[5] offered me a glimpse of his identity as a gay person that did not play out more deeply until almost two months later.

More importantly, by "hanging out" with the Lao American students, I was able to observe the tensions, shifts, and contradictions in the negotiations of culture and identity within the particular historical and social context of Dynamic High. Lao American students such as Lori, Nikhong, Somkiat, and Phongsava, among others,[6] helped me to understand the inadequacy of our normative, cohesive, binary discourses about their identities as urban, immigrant students. In the following pages I explore the contradictions of their identities, guided by three central questions: (1) How do dominant discourses frame urban, immigrant students? (2) How are the identities of immigrant students partial, unresolved, and more complex than dominant representations? and (3) How is an understanding of "unresolved identities" important for thinking about curriculum and pedagogy? This ethnographic study highlights and represents the experiences of Lao American students as a case for understanding the experiences of immigrant students in general, and for understanding the way identity is constructed more broadly in U.S. schools and society (Lincoln & Guba, 1985; Stake, 1995).

However, my account of the conversations, observations, and experiences of Lao students, their peers, and teachers at Dynamic does not seek to reveal the truth, actuality, or the reality of "being there." Instead, as a looking back or "second glance" (Britzman, 2000, p. 30), this poststructuralist ethnography acknowledges that its representation of Lao American students is a site of crisis and doubt. Part of the predicament, as Britzman (2000) points out, is that "ethnography [is] both a set of practices and a set of discourses" (p. 28). And because language is partial, fractured by "what cannot be said precisely because of what is said, and of the impossible difference within what is said, what is intended, what is signified, what is repressed, what is taken and what remains" (Britzman, 2000, p. 28) in writing, reading, and understanding, ethnographic narratives in themselves are partial. Indeed, they are "fictions" (Clifford, 1988) and "tales" (Van Maanen, 1988; Wolf, 1992).

Telling Stories

Let me tell a story that comes easily for me. It is a story about Trina, a senior Lao American student who was one of my primary participants. From my time with Trina at Dynamic High, I learned that the problems that the discourses of urban dysfunction emphasize are real issues that she faced on a daily basis. Like many of the students at the school, Trina contended with various personal, economic, and environmental challenges in her pursuit of education. Trina's position at the social and economic margins required household survival strategies (Tapia, 1998) that do not conform to dominant standards of household economic structures.

In Trina's experience, working multiple jobs to pay for her needs has been a part of her life from a young age. For several months during my time at Dynamic she held three jobs. As Trina negotiated the demands of getting good grades at school and earning money to support herself, time was at the forefront of her mind. This is how she balanced school and work:

> *Trina:* Okay, when I had three jobs, I have a planner and I've been carrying my planner for like forever. It takes care of my clinic appointments and school and work. So what I do is first you never get into something that you know you can't complete. So I make sure I know that I'm gonna be able to work and get my homework and still earn a good

grade. So that's what I go for the job. You don't ever get yourself into a mess where you can't get out of.

Trina is able to navigate the myriad responsibilities of school and work with exceptional time management. As she advised, this meant that "you never get into something that you know can't complete." The planner that she carried around "forever" helped Trina to track and make use of all of her time. As a student who was conscientious about grades, an important part of good time management included allotting time to complete her homework:

> *Trina:* And then time-wise like certain jobs I'll start not right after school, but a little bit after school. Then I can do my homework during that time or before I go to bed or wake up early in the morning and do it. But usually I do all my work at school so then I don't have to do it at home.

At another point, she also talked about completing class assignments in spare moments during the school day: "While I go to class I'll listen at the same time. But if it's really nothing big or nothing new I'll work on something else but listen at the same time." More often than not, Trina was able to complete most of her assignments at school.

Trina used the money that she earned to purchase her own clothes and school supplies and to pay for other needs. The year before my research, she was able to save money from less than a year of work to buy a new Honda sport utility vehicle for her father. In the year of my research, she bought a used Acura for herself. Additionally, Trina shared that she was considering several investment options, including War Bonds and Certificates of Deposit. When I asked her why earning and saving money was important for her, she told me that she wanted something to fall back on in case she needed money: "Something there to back me up because I don't want to go bankrupt or broke or whatever. And if I do there'll be something on the side that will be there waiting for me, that I'll be able take out and use just in case." According to Trina, investment was a good option for her because she is "very patient, especially if it's about money. So [she]'ll leave it as long as [she] want[s] to."

Trina's experiences as a poor immigrant demanded a renegotiation and reconstruction of family and economic standards. She recreated household structures and helped contribute to the economic needs of her family. While the structures of middle- and upper-middle-class households are set up to have parents as heads of households and as purchasers of cars for youth, the economic marginalization of students like Trina required a re-creation of household structures where youth took care of household bills and purchased cars for parents. Trina was able to do all of this while maintaining good grades that put her on the school's "B Honor Roll" for both semesters.

This story was an "easy" story for me to tell for a few reasons. It was easy because I was able to highlight Trina's strength as she negotiated the institutions of school, work, and home. It raised the possibility for another understanding of student identities that includes the role of breadwinner and other major responsibilities. I was able to highlight the challenges Trina faced as a poor immigrant, while reinforcing her remarkable strength. This triumphant, "beating the odds" story underscored the exemplary work ethic that allowed Trina to achieve in school and help her family despite extraordinarily difficult circumstances.

And yet, this is not the story about Lao American immigrant students that I want to tell. For one, it does not sufficiently illuminate the complexity of Trina's identity. In order to tell a story that underscored the positive aspects of her life, I left out elements that were problematic (cf. Lubienski, 2003). In such a feel-good account there was no room to share contradictory details of her life, like the fact that she was a student in the Comprehensive Program—the lowest academic track at Dynamic High. Even though Trina was able to attain good grades, she did not want to attend a 4-year college because she believed a 2-year degree would give her a quicker payback. Within the easy story, there was no place for incongruities like the 24-year-old high school dropout who has been her boyfriend for over 2 years.

I want to tell a different story—a counterstory—to the ones that dominate our understandings of what it means to be an urban resident, immigrant, and student. I want to make visible the discourses that are deployed by ourselves and by others in the process of identity-making that constrain and delegitimize the identity claims of students. Nonetheless, there are difficulties in telling stories about culture and identity. For one, as other ethnographers have done, I want to acknowledge the difficulty in "writing culture" (Clifford & Marcus, 1986). There is a contradiction in my desire to reveal the fluidity of culture and the act of writing—attempting to "freeze" culture on paper. Writing about the identity negotiations between Lao American students and their peers and teachers essentially involves trying to capture culture in-the-making. This ethnographic telling, then, is an incomplete snapshot of the lives of students, teachers, and staff at Dynamic High. What I describe in the following pages are fragments of stories of what happened within a specific context and time—a time that was already passé even as I was sitting with the students jotting down notes.

What I pass on in this book is my story or interpretation of the experiences of students and staff that I observed at Dynamic High. As I do so, I will present the words or voices of the experiences of my participants. Telling stories with the voices of others is a tricky undertaking, entangled with moral and epistemological implications. As feminist researchers (e.g., Fine, 1994b; Reinharz, 1992; Scott, 1992) suggest, we cannot represent the voices (of experience) as if they "speak for themselves" and are transparent proof of our research arguments. The voices that we collect from research participants are "interpretation[s] in need of an interpretation," (Scott, 1992, p. 37) which must be contextualized and historicized. The problem with using voices, then, is not that researchers edit and select voices in making their arguments. The trouble is that researchers rarely admit that we edit, interpret, translate, and choose—but pretend that we are not politically involved (Britzman, 2000; Fine, 1994b; Scott, 1992). My presentation—rather, re-presentation—of the experiences of Lao American students is by no means a "literal representation" or "mirror" of reality (Britzman, 2000), but is infused with my identity, interpretations, experiences, and politics.

Moreover, the stories I tell in this book about urban, immigrant identities engage writing strategies that highlight our discursive practices and trouble our belief in the "real" of culture and identity. As an attempt to shift the way we think and speak about urban, immigrant identities, my stories do not seek to make radical changes to our narrative conventions (Kondo, 1990; Weedon, 1987). However, following Kondo (1990), I believe that by spotlighting the "potential conflict, ambiguity, irony, and the workings of power in the very process of constructing identities could yield other insights and other rhetorical strategies to explore" (p. 304). Further, as an incomplete account of the lives of urban, immigrant students at Dynamic High, this ethnography, like all texts, contains inconsistencies, silences, and evidence of the limits of language (Weedon, 1987). The storylines in my narrative describe fragments of lives, and are in themselves replete with gaps and contradictions. Rather than produce "smooth stories of the self" (MacLure, 1996, p. 283) or arrive at a resolution in this book, I seek to emphasize the partialness of the stories we tell and write toward an "always more to the story" (Britzman, 1998, p. 321).

Lastly, there are tensions in aiming to reveal the influence and power of discourses while telling stories to accomplish the task. Just as I

expose and explain the discourses that frame and shape the identities of
Lao American students, I also draw on and deploy discourses to do so.
I am implicated in the same discursive process that I wish to spotlight.
The issue is not that we draw on discourses to make meaning. Rather,
the problems lie with the ways prevailing discourses simplify and confine
identities and pretend that they are naturally-occurring. What I want
to do is tell a story that brings attention to the hegemony of some
discourses and opens up possibilities for alternative identifications. As
Britzman (2000) advocates, ethnographic accounts should seek to

> trace how power circulates and surprises, theorize how
> subjects spring from the discourses that incite them, and
> question the belief in representation even as one must
> practice representation as a way to intervene critically in
> the constitutive constraints of discourses (p. 38).

Just as my ethnography is an attempt to resignify our current representations that confine and misrecognize urban, immigrant students,
my account is itself a representation that should be questioned. The
"doubleness" of this project (Gonick, 2003, p. 16), of highlighting the
way discursive practices constrain student identities while also deploying
discursive practices to create new identities, is a delicate undertaking.
Indeed, my project runs the risk of reinscribing the very discourses that
I want to unsettle. Nevertheless, such uncertainty and messiness are part
of the story that I want to tell. As the following chapters demonstrate,
even though we strive for cohesion and tidiness in the stories we tell
about ourselves and others, the fractures remain.

Things to Come

In the following chapters I elucidate the various discourses and practices that inform and shape the experiences and identities of urban,
Lao American high school students. I explore the ways that immigrant
youth identities are shaped by dominant discourses as well as the
ways that they modify, resist, or echo these discourses. I show that
while urban, Lao American students are changing what it means to
be "urban" and "immigrant" youth, most people are unable to read
them as doing so, and instead see the students as confused, backward,
and problematic.

   This introductory chapter examined the dominant representations
of urban, immigrant identities, and reviewed the bodies of literature
and epistemological perspectives that informed the study, analysis,

and writing. Chapters 2 through 5 illustrate the ways urban residents and students are placed in subject positions by available, controlling discourses and the ways students take subject positions by also drawing on available discourses. In different ways, these chapters pay attention to the role of discourses in meaning-making and in the construction of urban, immigrant identities. I begin broadly, by focusing on dominant understandings of urban education. This is important, because discourses about urban schools and urban students in general also contribute to the discourses about urban, immigrant students. Specifically, in Chapters 2 and 3, I examine discourses about Dynamic High School and its students, respectively. I focus on broader understandings about the urban school in general and elucidate the ways in which the dominant discourses were reflected in the stories about Dynamic High and its students. I specifically draw on document research about the school and conversations I had with teachers and staff. In these chapters, I explore the framing of the urban school and urban students as dysfunctional and failing by dominant discourses about what it means to live, teach, and learn in the city. I reveal the problematic tendency to understand and represent urban life and education within binary oppositions—for example, as passing/failing, good/bad, or functional/dysfunctional.

In Chapters 4 and 5, I focus on the experiences of Lao American students to complicate the dominant discourses about urban, immigrant students. Chapter 4 examines discourses about race and ethnicity as it relates to the identities of Lao American students at Dynamic High. I demonstrate the ways in which school discourses and practices lump and racialize Lao students as "Chinese" or "Hmong." To unsettle the cohesiveness of identity, I focus on the disagreements over the identities of Lao American students, as they and others draw on multiple, competing discourses in identity construction. Drawing on the stories of two Lao students, Lori and Mindy, I illustrate the interethnic and intraethnic tensions between Lao and Hmong students that are masked by the incongruities created in the double movement of identity.

Chapter 5 elucidates the partial, antagonistic, and fractured—ambivalent—characteristics of urban, immigrant identities. I draw on case studies of three Lao American students, whom I call Chintana, Kett and Vonechai, to explicate the range of discourses that Lao students invoke in their identity work. By illuminating the incongruous and precarious identities that the students produce in their identifications, I underscore the contradictory, multiple layers of identity.

Chapter 6 engages readers in a discussion about what it means to understand and theorize ambivalent, urban immigrant identities. I revisit the deficit discourses that teachers and staff used to make sense of the lives and experiences of their Lao American students to highlight the contradictions of their understandings. I do so to argue that, similar to students, the identities of teachers and staff were also uncertain and inconsistent. As such, they cannot be distilled into cohesive, dualisms of "bad, racist teacher" or "good, anti-racist teacher." Pointing to ways forward, I also examine the implications of my research for teaching, learning, and curriculum. I explicate the ways in which the experiences of my participants may provide insight into understandings about immigrant culture and multicultural pedagogy. I particularly explore what it means for pedagogical practices to conceptualize urban, immigrant identities as contradictory, fractured, and unresolved.

2

Urban Schools as War Zones

Many people sort of look to Dynamic as being sort of this model
school in Lakes City. It's the proverbial rags to riches or last to
first sort of thing. Dynamic all through the late 80s and early 90s,
Dynamic was sort of the running joke of the district. It was sort of
like being sent to Siberia (laughs). Teaching at Dynamic was like
the dregs of teaching in Lakes City Public Schools.

—Mr. Sullivan, English Teacher

Urban school films such as *Blackboard Jungle* (1955), *Stand and Deliver*
(1987), *The Principal* (1987), *Teachers* (1984), *Lean on Me* (1989), *Dangerous Minds* (1995), and *The Substitute* (1996) tell a particular story
about urban schools and urban students. In these films, students are
stereotypically portrayed as loud, violent, uncontrollable miscreants. The
schools are dirty, with hallways and classrooms marred by garbage and
graffiti. The overriding image of urban schools is that of an untamed
"jungle" or "war zone." The film *Lean on Me* (1989), starring Morgan
Freeman, exemplifies this dominant discourse. As we are introduced
to the students of Eastside High School in the opening scene, the
metaphor of the school as jungle is also established. We see students
being loud, assaulting teachers, harassing females, and selling drugs.
The chaos is emphasized by a soundtrack of Guns 'n Roses' angry,
shrill "Welcome to the Jungle." In this depiction, urban students are
the "animals"—wild and dangerous. As the movie progresses we learn
that the school is in danger of being placed in state control due to its
low basic skills test scores.

Such stories about urban education legitimate a certain discourse,
and influence how we think about urban schools, teachers, and students.
As I share below, the stories about Dynamic High and its students that
circulated inside and outside the school predominantly echoed the
images of popular Hollywood films. Drawing on conversations with
teachers and staff as well as stories from the local paper, I illuminate the
influence of dominant discourses on teacher and staff understandings

23

of the school. At the same time, I point to discrepant observations that
muddle normative characterizations of urban schools.

From Rags to Riches

Approximately ten years ago, Dynamic High was much like the Eastside High School of movies like *Lean on Me*. According to teachers
and staff, the school has a "mythical" reputation in the district and
state for transforming itself from the worst school to one of the top
high schools in the district. In the early 1990s neither teachers nor
students wanted to be at Dynamic. Due to low enrollment numbers
(approximately 600 students), the superintendent considered closing
the high school. Of this small number of students, roughly 450 would
show up on any given day. As a result of the low enrollment and low
attendance of students, entire wings of the three-story building were
not being used. The reputation of the school and the morale of the
students, teachers, and staff were so dismal that the joke around the
district was that students and teachers were sent to the school because
nobody else wanted them. Mr. Rogers, an assistant principal, shared,
"Administrators from other buildings joke about how ten years ago
on a bad day they would say, 'Well at least we're not at Dynamic.' "
Ms. Kane, an ELL (English Language Learner) teacher, reiterated
this account: "At one time this was a dumping ground school, a sort
of like backwater school. The school where the kids had failed and
been kicked out of other high schools they'd send them here." And
according to Mr. Sullivan, an English teacher, Dynamic was the "running joke of the district." Being placed in the school "was sort of like
being sent to Siberia" and "teaching at Dynamic was like the dregs of
teaching in the Lakes City Public Schools."
     At the height of the school's trouble period, Ms. Sanders began
her teaching career as an English teacher at Dynamic High. Within
4 years, due to rapid teacher turn-over she transitioned from being a
novice teacher to the chair of the English department. Her account
of the untenable situation at the school during this time is worth
quoting at length:

> *Ms. Sanders*: Ten years ago when I started here, for the
> most part morale was very, very low. Now I'll qualify that in
> a second, but I mean people said—I'm sure you've heard
> this before. People said, if you got in trouble, somebody
> would say, "So what? What are they going to do, send me

to Dynamic?" I mean *it was the worst place to be and everybody knew they were at the worst place in the whole city.* Kids didn't want to be here. They all said, "I want to go to [another school] this school's sorry, this school sucks." Attendance was terrible. Like maybe 60 to 70% attendance on any given day. Plus we didn't have that many kids to begin with. I think our population was five to seven hundred kids. We're fourteen-, thirteen-, fifteen hundred now. So it was kind of empty. It was kind of a ghost. I mean it was haunted. It was sort of creepy. Teachers left. Within my first 3 years I went from being the newest English teacher to the second in seniority in the English department. So by my 4th year I was chairing the department because I had more experience than anybody else. People couldn't wait to get out. Test scores were terrible. They were going to close the school. The superintendent was talking about closing the school, a lot of gang activity. We had no control of behavior, none.

BN: What do you mean?

Ms. Sanders: Oh, kids just you know, 'F You.' What were we going to do? Fights all the time. I mean I remember standing in front of a group of 10th graders and these kids just were like, "We're not doing anything." And I was a brand new teacher. I just didn't know what to do (laughs). They were throwing stuff out the window (laughs). It was just, *it was kind of a zoo.* I'm not exaggerating, but I'm telling you a lot of the details you're getting in one picture. It sort of illustrates it. None of this stuff happened in one day, but it happened and it happened regularly. The last day of school, no kids would come, because nobody gave finals. Nobody gave finals. It didn't seem important. Kids would come around, kids would miss 40 days in a quarter and then they'd come around and say to teachers—and this used to happen—"Can I get my credits still?" And the teachers would say, I mean a lot of our teachers would say, "Okay, we'll figure something out." And, I mean there were no standards. But we didn't know what we were about. It was really, it was pretty dismal. . . . It was terrible. I mean nobody wanted—You're looking at the hardest place to teach in the whole wide world (my emphasis).

Ms. Sanders' description of Dynamic High in the early 1990s invokes visions of urban education as reflected in popular discourse. Her account echoes themes portrayed by popular films such as *Dangerous Minds* (1995), *Lean on Me* (1989), and *Blackboard Jungle* (1955) where the authority of teachers and education are undermined both by student misbehavior, violence, and cynicism and by the low expectations of teachers for student achievement. Ms. Sanders' description of the school as a "kind of a zoo" dominated by gang violence, where students cursed at teachers and refused to do work, summons movie metaphors of the urban school as a "jungle" where the "student-animals" rule.

This storyline of urban school problems at Dynamic High was inscribed by the Lakes City newspaper. The paper reported, for example, that in November 1989, after a series of incidents where students were assaulted by other students, several dozen students threatened to walk out in protest because they wanted a safe school. A few years later, in 1992, students invited Theodore R. Sizer, renowned school reform scholar to their school. They wanted to hear how his Coalition of Essential Schools helped transform schools in Harlem, New York into places of order and learning. As the news story observed, during his visit, "Sizer was surrounded by the reality of a city classroom: bright kids sitting next to kids with learning disabilities, boys who hide their brains with macho urban chatter, girls silenced by lack of self-confidence, teenagers who desperately work for diplomas, loungers who watch the minutes tick by." Reiterating themes of urban menace, a 1993 story about school and community violence also reported: "Signs of our violent times are evident at Dynamic High School, starting with the fact that there's only one door you can enter at the school. All others are locked, to protect the students from the terror around them."

Similar to the narratives of teachers and staff, these newspaper accounts emphasize and repeat images of the violence and dysfunction at the school and in the community. These discourses combine to present a unitary understanding of the urban high school. Only occasionally, and as we will see in Chapter 3, this coherent storyline is interrupted by stories of triumph. According to the above, "the reality of the city classroom" includes common binary oppositions such as smart students and not-smart students, students who are overconfident and students who lack confidence, and hardworking students and lazy students. These prevailing accounts of Dynamic High echo and re-present Hollywood's urban school scripts. The themes of urban school problems such as poor attendance, out-of-control students, low standards, and gang activities that we see in movies such as *Lean on Me* are repeated in the story about Dynamic High School before its transformation.

In the movies, we often see urban schools and students converted or saved through the efforts of a single administrator or teacher. Michelle Pfeiffer's role in *Dangerous Minds* (1995) and Hilary Swank's more recent role in *The Freedom Writers* (2007) readily come to mind. In *Lean on Me* (1989), for example, Principal Joe Clark is able to turn Eastside High into a successful school within the single academic year in which the movie takes place. We see the early scenes of litter and graffiti that opened the movie transformed into gleaming floors and neatly organized classrooms. By the end of the movie Clark is able to make over the student body emotionally and intellectually. The disrespect and disdain that the students initially exhibited give way to school spirit and a rallying support of the principal at a school board meeting. By the conclusion of the movie, the low basic skills exam test scores are replaced by passing marks. For the finale, Clark leads the student body in a triumphant singing of the school anthem.

Resounding this storyline, teachers and staff told me that over a period of 8 years and under the leadership of two principals, Dynamic transformed from a school where neither students nor teachers wanted to be into a school with one of the top attendance rates and where teachers loved to teach. As Ms. Evans, a Civics teacher, observed:

> *Ms. Evans:* It's a great school as far as the staff is concerned. . . . We have a really good mix of people and personalities and talents and abilities, which I think makes the school thrive. I think the kids overall like their school and are proud to be here, and have a lot of school spirit.

Similar to the Eastside High of *Lean on Me*, the scorn for Dynamic by teachers and students changed to pride. The account of students with "a lot of school spirit" evokes images of Principal Clark and his students singing the school song. The dramatic metamorphosis of the school was characterized by Mr. Sullivan as a "proverbial rags to riches" story: "Right now many people sort of look to Dynamic as being sort of this model school in Lakes City. I mean we were—it's the proverbial rags to riches or last [place] to first [place] sort of thing."

While dominant discourses reify urban school triumph within tidy, feel-good accounts, what Mr. Sullivan characterized as the "rags to riches" transformation was painstakingly negotiated, messy, and difficult. Unlike the movies, the transition of Dynamic High into a "model school" did not occur overnight. The alteration took almost 10 years and 2 principals to reach its mythical status. It began with one principal who was at the school for 2 years; but much of the change occurred under the leadership of the current principal, Mr. Gibson. His account of the work that was involved in the transition muddies and disrupts the Hollywood-like story of Dynamic's evolution.

According to Mr. Gibson, the metamorphosis of the school is due in large part to a focused development of three capacities. First, Dynamic teachers and staff focused on the development of a positive student culture. He wanted students to "be proud of where [they] go to school, be proud of where [they] live, and really focused on getting kids engaged more in their school." Two ways in which the school invested in building this capacity included hiring a Student Support Services Coordinator and establishing a student government.[1] Second, Mr. Gibson worked to enhance teacher quality at the school. The establishment of the Professional Practice School[2] and the emphasis on and support for teachers attaining National Board Certification were especially important components of teacher quality enhancement activities. As Ms. Sanders explained, "Board Certification is to teaching what the bar exam is to lawyers, except it's voluntary." During my time at Dynamic, 4% of the Board Certified teachers in the state taught at the school. Third and finally, Mr. Gibson emphasized the importance of the school's involvement in the surrounding residential and business community. This included connecting with community and "cultural organizations" as well as attending community events and meetings. These activities were important for building the external capacities of the school, such as support services for students and keeping in touch with events in their home communities.

The effectiveness of the programs and organizational structures implemented by Mr. Gibson and his staff produced local and national attention that underscored the extraordinary "beat the odds" success of the school. In 2006, for example, the city paper reported that Dynamic High ranked first among all city high schools on state reading tests for low-income students, and second citywide for the state math tests. The story also highlighted that Dynamic equaled or outperformed some suburban high schools in the area. Today, the school Website boasts that it has the highest number of Nationally Board Certified teachers in the state and "has been named by *Newsweek* magazine as one of 'America's Best High Schools' in 2000, 2003, 2005, and 2006."

We Have a Million Languages

Despite accounts of its transformation into a "model" school, Dynamic still had an identity as a rough, "inner-city" school. One major contributing factor is its location in an industrial part of the city that was home to mostly African American and White American poor and working-class families. The particular region of the city, which I call the West Side,[3] is considered the most dangerous in the metropolitan area, with the highest crime rates in Lakes City. In 2001, for example, city crime statistics report that 24% of all crimes were committed in the area surrounding the school. This included 20 out of 43–46.5%—of the total homicides that occurred in the city. News accounts contributed to this sinister reputation by inscribing into the public imagination messages about shootings, murders, assaults, and gang activity. Headlines during the 2001–2002 period of my research included: "Man charged with arson in west Lakes City fire," "Man surrenders in west Lakes City killing," and "Gang killings may be on rise: Police are stepping up patrols and trying to sort out spate of killing in west Lakes City." In 2008, headlines still read: "A bloody weekend leaves two dead in west Lakes City" and "Man killed in west Lakes City after a fight over his girlfriend."

Despite such violent accounts, the neighborhood was not so one-dimensional. In contrast to the riotous reputation of the West Side, the locale of the school was in fact a very clean, quiet, residential neighborhood. Small, neat coffee shops and a few empty storefronts intermixed with unkempt and well-kept lawns. Homes in the immediate area surrounding the school included modest Craftsman bungalows and Tudors, built primarily between 1909 and 1932 for the workers in the nearby rail yard, grain mills, and sawmills. As more African American and Asian American families moved into the neighborhood, the student body of Dynamic High changed to reflect the residents. School records indicated that enrollment of students of color was 6% in 1976, 61% in 1991, and over 81% in 2001. While the school drew students from across the city because of its prestigious, college preparatory International Baccalaureate magnet program;[4] the enrollment of approximately 1,482 students was reflective of the racial and economic makeup of the neighborhood. The majority of the students were African American (43%), Asian American (38%) and White American (16%). Dynamic was also the poorest of the seven high schools in Lakes City, with 75% of its student body receiving free or reduced lunch.[5]

Taken together, the location and student demographics meant that Dynamic continued to be identified as a problematic urban, public high school. As Mr. Rogers put it, Dynamic High was "still an inner-city school":

> *Mr. Rogers*: We get all kinds of staff people from around the district now who want to come here. This used to be the assignment of last resort for a lot of people. That's not so

any longer. But we're still an inner-city school. We're still dealing with *tremendous* issues of poverty, and everything that goes with that—multiple layer upon layer of issues that go with kids from generational poverty. So it's not an easy gig either. We haven't arrived—which is why I say it's a work in progress.

While the school was no longer viewed as the "assignment of last resort," due to the misbehavior and low achievement of its students, student characteristics continued to define the school. By and large, Mr. Rogers declared that Dynamic was still "not an easy gig" and defined it as an "inner-city school" because of its students. In the above remarks, Mr. Rogers alluded to the ways that poverty impacted the lives of students, their work in classrooms, and the work of teachers and staff at the school. However, as we will see in Chapter 3, this emphasis on the deprivation of the home life of students contradictorily re-inscribed discourses of urban dysfunction.

Like Mr. Rogers, the majority of the teachers and staff recognized that Dynamic High was "a work in progress." Through conversations with teachers and staff, I learned more about the features of an "inner-city school." For example, when I asked faculty and staff to describe the school, they invariably pointed to the "diversity" of the students. They talked about the many ways in which students were racially, ethnically, linguistically, academically, and economically diverse. Consider, for instance, the responses of some teachers when I asked them to describe the school:

> *Ms. Kane:* Describe Dynamic. As a large inner-city, urban school with the minority students as the majority here. We have every, we have students who speak, all over the building they speak around 40 different languages with the majority second language being spoken is Hmong and then Liberian standard English. Then we have some kids who, a few kids, who speak Lao and lots of others.

> *Ms. Sanders:* I'll start with diverse 'cause that's, I can start with the cliché, it's easier. I mean the languages obviously. We have a million languages that are spoken. . . . You've got a whole range of socioeconomics going on. A whole range of their ability to do school and their experience with school is vastly different. If you look at our White student population, I mean they come from [outside the community] where a

parent wants them, has this feel-good idea about keeping
their kid in the city school, not going to send them to private.
So they're picking a magnet program. And a neighborhood
kid who lives, who walks here from, you know, three blocks
away. I think they come from different places. . . . It's not just
different kinds of American kids. We get different kinds of
world kids. It's a cosmopolitan place that way. I think they
bring a vast range of experiences, good and bad.

As a way to describe the school, teachers appealed to the discourse—or
cliché—of diversity to highlight the myriad ways that students were
different. They pointed out that students came from various local and
global geographic places, spoke "a million languages," had different
preparation and expectations for education, came from dissimilar economic circumstances, and had a range of academic abilities.[6] As Ms.
Sanders described above, Dynamic High was "a cosmopolitan place"
with "different kinds of American kids" as well as "different kinds of
world kids." The framing of difference and "diversity" is particularly
noteworthy. On one hand, the diversity of the student body was positively positioned in the 2001–2002 school brochure, which painstakingly highlighted that the students and staff spoke 41 languages and
dialects. On the other hand, and as we will see in the next chapter,
the emphasis on "diversity" is much more insidious.

Do You Have Metal Detectors?

As teachers shared their experiences at Dynamic and the perception
of those from outside the school community, fractures appeared in
the smooth, binary accounts of the school as a problematic space of
failure or as a model of successful reform. While the teachers and
staff told a story of Dynamic that highlighted it as an improved yet
imperfect "work in progress," they also observed that their understanding of Dynamic conflicted with that of friends and acquaintances. Ms.
Evans, for instance, shared that when she tells people who are familiar
with Lakes City that she works at Dynamic High School, the response
includes gasps and exclamations of "Oh my God!" Her friends ask
"just dumb questions" such as "How are the kids? Can they read? Do
they care about the school, and are they smart?" In a similar vein, Ms.
Hanson, an English teacher, recounted that friends are surprised when
they learn that she teaches at Dynamic. Their questions include: "Are
you ever afraid?" "Do you have metal detectors?" "How many times
do your students fight in your classroom?" and "How many times do

you have lock downs?" These questions imply a certain understanding of urban life; and resound discourses that identify urban schools as places of violence, where teachers fear for their safety and metal detectors are necessary to locate concealed weapons. Indeed, the question about "lock downs" tellingly draws on language most frequently used to describe prison procedures for outbreaks of violence and mayhem. Taken together, these questions by acquaintances of Dynamic High teachers invoke widely circulated, normative notions of urban schools that position urban students as individuals who do not care about their schools, who do not even know how to read.

The perception that Dynamic High is a place of imminent risk draws on broader understandings about urban life as well as on specific discourses about the West Side neighborhood in which the school is located. As Ms. Evans insightfully commented, the remarks about students as failures and threats to safety are linked to the location of the school in the city in general, and to the West Side in particular. She noted that for teachers who work in suburban schools, "people are like, 'I've heard of the basketball team' or 'That sounds great,' or 'Wow, you're a teacher, neat.' But I have gotten some interesting comments about this school and working on the West Side." It is no coincidence that a school in an area of the city that is home to primarily poor African American families is discursively constituted as dangerous with students who do not know how to read. The public perception draws on and redeploys what Paul Gilroy (1991) has argued as a past where the mass exodus of African Americans from the south to northern cities fostered racist metaphors of the "city as jungle" to describe the homes of urban African Americans (p. 228). In the present day of Dynamic High, the discursive inscription of "urban" has perhaps become what Haymes (1995) argues as "another way to signify the 'evils' of blackness and black people" (p. 115).

Images and narratives of urban violence and underachievement are familiar and available to us in our meaning-making because they are circulated and legitimated repeatedly. School-bashing has long been a frequent theme in public discourse. In addition to popular films, the print news media repeat stories about the chaos and trouble that exist in urban schools. Sources such as *U.S. News and World Report* have told us that "school violence is on the rise" (Toch, Gest & Guttman, 1993); the *New York Times* reported, "In an Era of School Shootings, a New Drill" (Kelley, 2008); and *USA Today* recounted, "Big City Schools Struggle with Graduation Rates" (Toppo, 2006). And as we saw above, narratives about the problems of Dynamic High and the West Side neighborhood privilege a storyline of violence and dysfunction. For the teachers at Dynamic, the repetition of these discourses of urban crisis was a point of frustration. Mr. Sullivan, for instance, told me: "I'm so tired of war imagery and metaphors as far as teachers and students in the schools." Likewise, Ms. Jenkins, a Civics teacher at the school, shared her exasperation:

> *Ms. Jenkins*: I love Dynamic. When people ask me, "Where do you want to teach?" or "How do you like your job? Where would you want to teach, in the suburbs?" "No." I realize it's an urban school and it has a lot of urban issues. But I think I'm getting tired of people telling me it's an "inner-city school." . . . My sister oftentimes will introduce me, "Oh this is my sister, you know she teaches in the inner-city." And it's like, "Ooo" was the attitude. I think that just has kind of an opinion and attitude and judgments behind that.

People who ask Dynamic teachers "Where would you want to teach? In the suburbs?" assume that the evils of the "inner-city" school are such that if given the choice, teachers would choose suburban schools. In the public imagination, it is inconceivable that teachers would voluntary work at an urban school. As Ms. Jenkins shared, she's "getting tired of people telling [her] it's an inner-city school." Similarly, Ms. Hanson observed "that [there are] a lot of misconceptions or ideas about teaching in an urban environment" such as Dynamic. These comments about the attitudes and judgments toward urban schools convey an irritation with the overemphasis on the troubles of urban education. Here, we see murmurs of a critique of the dominant discourse of urban school problems. Nevertheless, as we will see in Chapter 3, teachers also contradictorily contribute to these simplistic notions of urban schools in their discursive construction of Dynamic High students.

Unraveling the Discourse of Urban Dysfunction

The story of Dynamic High School is, to a certain extent, the story of urban schools in general. It is a story that is discursively constructed, that draws on two available, dominant storylines of the urban school. What it means to be an urban school is constituted within simplistic dichotomies that highlight at one extreme, urban turmoil and underachievement, and at the other extreme, triumphant transformation. But as we saw, the transformative "success" of Dynamic's mythical "rags to riches" story was read differently by those from inside and those from outside the school. Teachers characterized the Dynamic High of the past and the Dynamic High of the present within different frameworks. Unlike other urban school narratives that illuminated a discursive tendency toward a romantic(ized) nostalgia of the past (see, e.g., Yon, 2000) the storylines that teachers and staff deployed about Dynamic did just the opposite. Teachers and staff did not talk about "the good old days" when the school was free of problems brought on by the diversity of cultures and interests. Rather, their stories emphasized a troubled school history of mythical proportions, which gave way to more "typical" characteristics of an urban school. While teachers and staff no longer considered the school to be a "zoo" or a "dumping ground," this narrative persisted in the public imagination. For community friends and acquaintances of the teachers, Dynamic continued to be the dangerous, chaotic urban jungle, characterized by metal detectors and violent students who do not want to learn. The negative public understanding and portrayal of urban schools were not lost on the teachers and staff at Dynamic. Their accounts revealed that they were acutely aware of the prevailing urban school-bashing discourses, and wanted to make counterclaims that qualified and pushed back against the overemphasis on urban school problems.

These inconsistent, conflictual understandings of Dynamic High (and the urban school in general) point to the presence of multiple, competing discourses. But these storylines are not just "out there," circulating harmlessly. The normative discursive frameworks of urban transformation, diversity (e.g., race, poverty, academic ability), and violence promote ideas about the urban school as essentially "bad," with rare occasions of redemption in which it is "good." The implication of essentializing and naturalizing urban schools and students as dangerous, violent, failures is the ideological positioning of urban students, teachers and schools as the source of the problems in urban public education. This problematic identification of urban-ness with dysfunction provides a justification for punitive responses in the homes, schools, and communities of low-income students and families of color. As Thomas West (2002) persuasively argues:

> The idea of culture-as-civilization historically has equated civility with politically and morally "mature" cultures and uncivility with "savagery" or politically and morally "immature" or "backward" cultures, thereby relegating them to the nonpolitical, to a culture justifiably dealt with by means outside "civil" politics—by violence, oppression or occupation, for instance (p. 115).

Discursively constituted through jungle metaphors, students and teachers are the unruly "savages" or "animals" that must be controlled.

In poor, urban communities today, disciplinary practices stemming from the notion that urban schools are immature and uncivilized have materialized in the forms of accountability, standardized tests and "No Child Left Behind." In their analysis of California's curriculum standards, Sleeter and Stillman (2005) explore the connection of curriculum standards with broader power relationships. They contend, "standards fit within a political movement to reconfigure power relations among racial, ethnic, language and class groupings" (p. 44). For Sleeter and Stillman, the accountability movement is "not simply about trying to improve student learning, but more important, about reasserting who has a right to define what schools are for [and] whose knowledge has most legitimacy" (p. 44). Arguably, urban schools and communities, populated primarily by immigrant and other students of color are being told that their values, knowledges, and identities are illegitimate and backward, if not altogether "uncivil."

As we turn to discourses about urban students in the next chapter, we see the particular ways that the urban students and families at Dynamic High were delegitimized and positioned as unstable, undisciplined—uncivilized.

3

War Babies and Comeback Kids

Well, I think as far as the demographics, it's a very diverse school. About approximately 40% African American, 40% Asian, 20% Caucasian. Also diverse, pretty diverse academically. We have students who have a lot of needs. You know we have everything from the ELL kids who have, like, limited formal schooling, never been to school, and all the way up to the IB. You know, so there's real diversity.

—Ms. Anderson, ELL Teacher

From the perspective of Ms. Anderson, Dynamic High School was diverse because of its students. Diversity at the school was "real" because of the varying racial and ethnic backgrounds, language proficiencies, and academic abilities of the student body. The assertion of the "real diversity" at the school begs the question: What is "real" about the diversity at Dynamic? In relation: What is "fake" or "not-so-real" diversity? The remark about "students who have a lot of needs" suggests a seriousness to "real diversity" that contrasts with the "celebrate diversity" of multicultural education and its "trivial examples and artifacts of cultures such as eating ethnic or cultural foods, singing songs or dancing, [and/or] reading folktales" (Ladson-Billings & Tate, 1995, p. 61). Lubienski (2003) provides an exceptionally cogent analysis of this overemphasis on cheerful or "not real" diversity. According to Lubienski, for the past several decades, educational and other social science research on poor, urban families (particularly African American families) have put an overemphasis on the *positive* aspects of diversity. The diversity of ethnic and language traditions of groups has been favored in research with minoritized populations, to the almost complete denial of economic disparities (Lubienski, 2003; Wilson, 1991). Ignoring the seriousness of diversity has meant disregarding problems such as domestic violence, malnutrition, and substance abuse.

As Lubienski (2003) persuasively argues, the shift to the focus on "celebrating diversity" in research is linked to the negative response to government-sponsored research for affirmative action programs. Moynihan's (1965) work, for instance, sought to elucidate racial and class inequalities, and to establish programs such as Head Start. However, and ironically, his illumination of the "culture of poverty"—crime, drug abuse, single parents, and school dropouts—of urban, African American communities was intensely criticized as Anglo-centric, culturally biased, "blame-the-victim" research (Lubienski, 2003). Moynihan received scathing condemnation even though he pointed to the contributing roles of urbanization, unemployment, and "three centuries of exploitation" (Rainwater & Yancey, 1967, p. 5) to the problems faced by African American families. The response of the research community to the backlash against "culture of poverty" research was to "ground to a halt" (Wilson, 1991, p. 593) studies that focused on the negative issues facing poor, urban communities (Lubienski, 2003).

What remains of this controversy are two normative discourses about poor, urban identities. One narrative invokes the "culture of poverty" research by negatively pointing to the self-made problems of poor, urban communities. The other storyline appeals to the success stories of "celebrate diversity" initiatives that stress resilience, perseverance, and triumph despite inequitable conditions and resources. The dominance of these two narratives has created binary oppositions for making sense of urban identities. It has thus been difficult to talk about the disparities of urban experiences outside of these two simplifying, confining storylines. In this chapter, I elucidate the ways teachers and staff made sense of their students through discourses that framed urban students as "war babies" who come from unstable homes, but who are sometimes able to become "comeback kids." Even as I highlight their discourses—which at times do not reflect well on the teachers and staff—I also recognize the inadequacy of my own words to illustrate the complexity of their experiences and intentions. To be sure, I was an outsider to Dynamic, without the enormous responsibilities of teaching and meeting standards, among other complications that are part of the day-to-day realities of the teachers and staff.

"They Are War Babies"

> For some, the Bible is the only book at home. Many struggle with absent parents. One day, when her class finished an assignment early, someone pulled up the state corrections department Website. Almost everyone had a parent or uncle to look up. One girl searched in vain for her father's mug shot; she's never seen him.
>
> —Lakes City newspaper story about Dynamic students, 2006

In many ways, the students at Dynamic personified images depicted by the discourse of urban dysfunction. When students walked through the front doors of the school they also brought into the hallways and classrooms the effects of their social and economic marginalization. Poverty was not an isolable entity that could be easily taken off and stowed away in lockers. Instead, poverty and its effects were interwoven into the daily process of learning, teaching, and living. Recall the way Mr. Rogers described Dynamic and the emphasis that he put on the impact of poverty: "But we're still an inner-city school. We're still dealing with *tremendous* issues of poverty, and everything that goes with that—multiple layer upon layer of issues that go with kids from generational poverty." As Mr. Rogers explained, the poverty of the students at Dynamic was unlike what "the average middle-class American probably thinks of poverty." Poverty for his students is "far more complicated" than not having money; it includes substance and physical abuse, broken homes, and "a general despair of people who don't particularly feel like they have a stake in this society."

For urban schools like Dynamic, poverty had profound implications for teaching and learning. Mr. Gibson, the school principal, observed:

> *Mr. Gibson:* Now you can focus on your teaching and instructing and make sure that you have a curriculum that is up to speed. You have qualified staff; [you can] work on having kids come every day. But outside of that, there's really not a lot you can deal with in terms of the lives of students and families. And when you have a building that has a high level of poverty as we do, poverty does have that impact on families and their ability to cope with a variety of things. You have things like adult literacy issues for non-English speaking parents, a whole range of things.

From Mr. Gibson's perspective, he and the rest of his staff have influence over teacher preparation, curricula, and policies about attendance and behavior. However, it was more difficult to control and address what goes on in the homes of students and the way poverty affects the way families "cope with a variety of things."

Dynamic High teachers and staff made sense of the impact of urban poverty on their students and the "whole range of things" that are part of urban life by drawing on images of war. Ms. Sanders, for example, described her urban, immigrant students as "damaged" and

as "war babies" by recounting the description of a visiting poet who
taught at Dynamic for a few weeks:

> *Ms. Sanders*: We had a poet here, and it was interesting. He
> wrote a report about his experience here and he talked. . . . I
> think *he calls them war babies*. And he's right in a way. *They're
> damaged you know*. So many of them, I think, just have had
> so much damage done to them. When you're sitting down
> with a kid, you really see that kind of stuff a lot. . . . I sat
> down with a kid yesterday 'cause he had cheated on a
> paper. . . . And in some ways I was happy that he cared
> enough to get a paper in 'cause he hadn't turned in a
> paper most of the year. . . . I asked him, "How did you get
> to this point where you have to cheat on a paper? You don't
> need to. You write really well." And he said, "I don't have
> enough time . . . I'm living with my grandmother because
> my aunt kicked me out. And I don't know where to turn."
> And somebody shot his dog last week. He's taking the bus
> from [another city] to come here, and he's been kicked out
> of four schools in the last two years. Now they're looking
> at alternative school. He should be a senior, he's in a 10th
> grade class (my emphasis).

These words make real the challenges faced by the teachers and students at Dynamic High. Ms. Sanders' comments about how a student
cheated on a paper because he had to deal with being kicked out of
his aunt's house, commuting to school, and having his dog shot point
to the social and economic turbulence of urban life. The description
of the movement of the student between different homes alludes to
stories about "broken homes" and out-of-wedlock pregnancies. This
portrayal of what it means to be an urban student invokes metaphors
of "war zones" to describe urban communities, where students are "war
babies" who have been "damaged" by violence, abuse, and neglect.
The result is an exceptionally negative account of urban homes and
communities.

While Ms. Sanders referenced the metaphor of war to describe
the effects of poverty and home life on the students, Ms. Kane called
upon images of war to explain the influence of refugee experiences
to describe Dynamic students. As a teacher who primarily worked with
Lao, Hmong, and Liberian students, she underscored the salience of
posttraumatic scars that immigrant students bring to school:

Ms. Kane: If you have people who just come in from war situations, I mean some of them have been through the most horrible things and they may not talk about it in class, but they'll write them out in a story or if I make a generalization about, "Oh, I was really sad or I was upset when something happened, when I saw something happen." Then they would say, "Oh yeah, I saw something like that." You'll see it in—I remember a boy made a poster and you were supposed to write—it was just science—living things, nonliving things—basic. But he had nonliving, some very horrid-looking bodies from a war situation that he had put on his poster. And other people had rocks and fish and he had these kinds of mutilated, horrid-looking kind of things on part of his. And some of them are carrying, I think, great sadness inside. So I think that interferes.

Increasingly, urban schools such as Dynamic are dealing with issues that arise not only from extreme poverty, but also from territorial displacement and refugee resettlement. The Lakes City metropolitan area, for example, has seen a dramatic increase in war refugees from Lao, Hmong, Liberian, and Somali ethnic groups within the past 10 years. As a result, schools such as Dynamic are progressively dealing with postwar traumatic issues. Ms. Kane's "war babies" were not from the streets of the city, but from transnational ethnic and civil wars. The impact of these conflicts surfaced through illustrations of "horrid-looking bodies from a war situation." For Ms. Kane, these depictions provided evidence of the "great sadness" of emotional health issues that interfered with their education.

The emphasis on stories about gang activities, prostitution, malnutrition, and postwar trauma framed students as children of local and global wars. They were "war babies" of generational poverty and urban problems, and they were "war babies" of geopolitical dislocation and conflicts. The response of some teachers to the difficulties faced by their students was to make adjustments to curriculum and pedagogy. As Ms. Sanders shared, this meant taking on more than just an identity as a teacher:

Ms. Sanders: Well I think our kids come with just a range of needs. The cliché right now is about schools needing to satisfy home life things that aren't being satisfied. So we're social workers, we're parents. There's that cliché that

schools are being asked to do everything. I think that's true
everywhere. I think it's more true when you have a student
population like ours where the kids are coming not necessarily ready to do school. A lot of them not knowing how
to do school in many ways, not having breakfast, not having
somebody at home necessarily [who] cares about that, not
having books at home.

Significantly, the day-to-day work of urban teachers is more complex
than teaching English grammar or math theorems. In addition to
responsibilities for teaching, learning, and meeting testing standards,
Ms. Sanders shared that "schools are being asked to do everything."
In this remark, Ms. Sanders underscored for us the intensification of
the work of teachers (Apple, 2000). But further, the way that she positioned students and families is also noteworthy. Teachers and school
staff must take on roles as parents and social workers because "home
life things aren't being satisfied." Here, students have a "range of
needs" because they "may not know how to do school," may not have
had breakfast, books at home, or "somebody at home [who] necessarily cares." These words draw on negative depictions of urban families,
pointing to the failure of parents and family for the circumstances of
Dynamic students.

As other teachers and staff repeated, outside school conflicts also
affected the contexts for teaching and learning in other ways. According to Mr. Rogers, the home life of students had ramifications for their
behavior at Dynamic:

> *Mr. Rogers:* You definitely have to be aware of the fact that
> the kid sitting in the third row with his head down could
> have his head down for a variety of reasons other than just
> being defiant. Mom and her boyfriend may have been up
> all night fighting last night. That young man may not have
> gotten breakfast. Case in point—just this year one of our
> terrific kid's father died very suddenly, which threw him for
> a loop because that *was* the one stable figure in his life. I
> mean, there's all kinds of things that happen to these kids
> all the time. And you have to be attuned to it. I would say
> 95% of the time, when one of our kids goes off—gets angry,
> throws a fit, cussing somebody out. Most of the time they're
> not cussing out the teacher that's receiving the anger. Most
> of the time they're angry about something else and they're
> just, they're venting. They're busting out. Now is it appropri-

ate? No. If they do that on the job will they get fired? Yes.
So we still have to teach them that's inappropriate. But the
point is, where is that coming from? And often you have to
deal with where that anger is coming from before you can
teach Shakespeare.

Similar to Ms. Sanders, Mr. Rogers pointed to the way outside-school
issues affected inside-school experiences. He noted that the instability
of a home with a single "mom and her boyfriend who may have been
up all night fighting" translated in school to students making angry
outbursts and putting their heads down on desks. What happens at
home impinges on the work of teachers because they "have to deal
with where that anger is coming from before [they] can teach Shakespeare." Thus, when a student "goes off—gets angry, throws a fit, cussing
somebody out," it is a response to things that occurred at home rather
than to the actions of teachers. In this narrative, Mr. Rogers deflected
blame for student misbehavior from teachers and students themselves.
Instead, parents and the problems of the urban household—of "mom
and her boyfriend" rather than "mom and dad"—are the culprits.
Paradoxically, in his attempt to challenge storylines about uncontrollable urban students and schools, Mr. Rogers reinscribed discourses of
urban home turmoil.

At the same time that teachers and staff must be aware of family and community issues, they also must figure out when and how to
challenge their students academically. The delicacy of this task was
conveyed by Ms. Anderson in this way:

> *Ms. Anderson*: It was horrible. Yeah, their hair was like all
> patchy and stuff you know. So there's stuff like that. . . . And
> a lot of times you don't know for sure, but you realize
> that "Okay, this kid is here today and usually they're pretty
> positive or wide awake" or whatever it is, and today they're
> really surly and cranky or they have their head down or
> something. And trying to figure out "Okay, well, how hard
> do I push this kid? Is there something going on outside that
> I don't know about?"

The students that Ms. Anderson saw in her classroom had hair that had
fallen out as well as difficulties "going on outside" in their homes. The
inconsistency of their attitudes, alertness, and crankiness had implications for her work as a teacher. As Ms. Anderson put it, she needed
to ask herself, "[H]ow hard do I push this kid?"

Teachers and staff like Ms. Anderson, Mr. Rogers, and Ms. Sanders invoked deficit, "culture of poverty" discourses to make sense of what it means to be an urban resident. By drawing on available, normative storylines of urban dysfunction to understand students and families, they simplified and limited the possibilities for alternative identifications. And yet, the identities of teachers and staff are not cohesive as uncaring, "bad" adults. Ms. Anderson's pedagogical considerations of the mood of students and desire to "push" her students suggest a more complex, ambivalent identity. Likewise, Mr. Rogers was adamant about having high expectations for Dynamic High students. Within moments of the above remarks that criticized the instability of urban home life, he asserted that even though students come from difficult circumstances, "it doesn't mean we have to make excuses for them. It doesn't mean we let them off because they've had a hard life. If we do that, we're cheating them." In framing the identities of his urban students, Mr. Rogers deployed conflicting discourses—one that maligned their families and another that underscored his concern for them.

Similar to Ms. Anderson and Mr. Rogers, Ms. Sanders also worried about the academic well-being of her students. She explained her teaching efforts in this way:

> *Ms. Sanders:* We're dealing with a lot of factors that really affect our kids. So those are real challenges because that's a student's circumstances. I don't want to necessarily say, "Well that's your lot in life then." My goal is to say that this kid has the same opportunities as a kid who's going to [a wealthy suburban school]. I've got more work to do. We've got more work to do but that's our challenge is to say, "You can. If you choose, you can compete with that kid."

Despite calling upon negative images of urban problems to frame the lives and identities of students, teachers also cared a great deal about their students. Ms. Anderson, Mr. Rogers, and Ms. Sanders wanted a lot for Dynamic students. As Ms. Sanders remarked above, as a teacher she cannot simply tell students "That's your lot in life" and accept that her students cannot have the same opportunities as wealthy students. Instead, it means that as an urban schoolteacher she must do more to provide students from a low-income background with "the same opportunities as a kid" from an affluent background. Importantly, the discursive practices of Dynamic High teachers and staff are complex. Just as their discourses portray urban families negatively, they simultaneously express deep care for students. I suggest that it would be difficult to label them as "good" or "bad." The implication for teachers and staff is that their identities are also uncertain and non-unitary. I return to elucidate the ambivalence of teacher identities further in Chapter 6.

School as Shelter

Alongside the framing of Dynamic High students as "war babies" were ideas about urban homes and neighborhoods as "war zones" or "jungles." In the war zone, students "battled" daily situations that included absentee parents, gang activities, prostitution, and malnutrition. As teachers and staff discursively constituted student identities as "war babies" of urban and global warfare, they also positioned the school as a shelter from the disorder and violence. Repeatedly, teachers and staff focused on the instability of homes in the urban "war zone." Consider what Mr. Rogers said about students and their "desperate need and desire for structure."

> *Mr. Rogers*: With a lot of our kids there's a *desperate need and desire for structure which they lack*, many of them, in their home lives. It was certainly my experience in teaching that some of the wildest kids at first really responded to structure, routine, knowing what was expected of them, and my not messing with the routine. If I messed with the routine it was disruptive, it was disturbing. *Our kids really react to being provided a sense of security*. That's why I think the behavior gets sort of wacky at the end of the year. I think a lot of kids sense that summer is coming; this *safe haven* here will be gone for 3 months. *And then it's back to 24/7 out in the community, out in the neighborhood, out on the streets, out on the courts.* And it's tough around here (my emphasis).

Swirling in the above is the juxtaposition between the stability of urban homes and urban schools. From Mr. Roger's perspective, students lacked constancy and routine in their home lives. In the spaces of Dynamic, students who at first are "the wildest kids" were able to calm down and responded positively to the routines of school and "knowing what was expected of them." As Mr. Rogers explained, if he veered from the routine, it was "disturbing" to the students. As a "safe haven," Dynamic "provided a sense of security" to its students for 9 months of the year. But then, according to Mr. Rogers, for the 3 months of summer, the stability is taken away and students were "back to 24/7 out in the community, out in the neighborhood, out on the streets, out on the

courts." Underneath these remarks are whispers about what it meant
to be in urban homes, neighborhoods, and playgrounds. They intone
messages of urban strife and turmoil where one would need to seek
"structure," "routine," "security," or a "safe haven" elsewhere.

In comparable language, Ms. Hanson positioned the school as a
source of shelter and continuity for students:

> *Ms. Hanson*: Things may be going on at home that we don't
> know about that could be affecting the child's ability to
> concentrate. So this wide range of home stability, skill level
> that they come into high school with, if they have any type
> of emotional or behavior problems, ESL students, students
> that are maybe moving around from different schools con-
> stantly. *They don't have that stable environment* of having one
> consistent place where they can learn. *They've been shuffled
> around and moved so much* that I think that they sometimes
> get lost in the system, in the public education system and the
> idea of open enrollment. *So I think a lot of our students suffer
> because they move so often or [have] attendance issues, which has to
> deal with things at home or illness.* I find a lot of students with
> serious health problems, I think, having to do with teach-
> ing in the city, asthma, and other issues. So I don't know.
> When I look at them as emotional beings and being able to
> establish relationships, they're really wonderful. They have
> really strong senses of humor. It's amazing how resilient they
> are even when you find out what's going on at home, how
> they can really let that go. And I think the *school sometimes
> is kind of a shelter* from that (my emphasis).

To be sure, this framing of the urban students at Dynamic High redeployed images and discourses of urban social pathology. Ms. Hanson's
remarks about "attendance issues, which has to deal with things at
home or illness" reiterate themes of health problems, troubled relationships, and responsibilities of youth at home. For Ms. Hanson, the
"students suffer" because "they've been shuffled around" by parents
and guardians. Her comment that "[i]t's amazing how resilient they
are even when you find out what's going on at home, how they can
really let that go" is significant for its double message. The "amazing"
strength of students is praised at the same time that their families and
community are condemned for "what's going on at home."

One of the ways Dynamic teachers and staff responded to the
"instability" of the urban home and neighborhood was to "create an

environment where the kids can spend a great deal of time." Mr. Sullivan explained the efforts of the school in this way:

> *Mr. Sullivan*: We've really made an effort here in realizing that *the school is in many senses probably the most consistent thing in many of these kids' lives.* To create an environment where the kids can spend a great deal of time here and be involved in many different things. Whether it be a book club, whether it be Chess Team, whether it be a sports team, whether it be some sort of a club or organization that puts together dances. Or even like the Asian Club or, you know, all of this. There are a number of places and opportunities for kids to become involved and to, in many senses, *create a surrogate family if you will that might not exist at home.* And from that standpoint, I'm not saying we're perfect at it and God knows we have our issues, but I think we've done a pretty good job of trying to expand that and sort of bring kids into that more and *make this more of a community meeting place*: the school itself as opposed to just the school that you go to for 6 hours, like a business (my emphasis).

Much like Mr. Rogers, Mr. Sullivan positioned the school as one of few places of consistency for his students. As he implied in the above account, the more students spent time at school involved in extracurricular activities, the more they were protected from the volatility of the streets. As a refuge from the havoc of city life, Dynamic was positioned as a "surrogate family" for students. According to Mr. Sullivan, teachers and staff sought to make Dynamic more than "just the school that you go to for 6 hours" and into one that was "more of a community meeting place."

Indeed, teachers shared that in school students are able to make connections and nurture each other in ways that they cannot do at home. They recounted stories of students who came to school just to socialize with friends. As teachers shared, students came into their classrooms without completed assignments or not prepared to pay attention, but yet they attended school on a regular basis. Ms. Hanson specifically discussed how students "disclose quite a bit to friends between classes and during their lunchtime and social time." Friendships among students provided them with confidantes with whom they shared experiences like crushes on classmates to more serious situations such as abuse at home. As Ms. Hanson remarked, "A lot of times friends will come to me and tell me what the situation is if the student isn't able to. Like the girl who was concerned about her friend getting abused . . . they do kind of look out for each other."

While teachers and staff such as Ms. Hanson, Mr. Rogers, and Mr. Sullivan redeployed discourses of urban dysfunction, they were also offering a new storyline to the narrative. Their positioning of urban schools as "safe havens" and "shelters" from the evils of urban homes and neighborhoods challenged the prevalent understanding of urban schools as "blackboard jungles" saturated by drug activities and gang violence. Instead, teachers and staff wanted to promote a discourse that highlighted the security and stability of the school. The construction of Dynamic High as a space of shelter and community-building resonates with the explication by Fine and Weis (1998) of the way urban schools may act as "free spaces." Their research with urban poor and working class young adults revealed that schools "offer sites wherein parents meet together, compare notes . . . negotiate day-to-day problems and begin to imagine and organize for 'what could be,' despite tough pasts and foreboding presents" (p. 243). Such efforts to open possibilities for alternative framings of schools are critically important for unsettling the dominance of simplistic, dichotomous categories.

However, by framing the homes and communities of their students as unstable and problematic, the teachers and staff at Dynamic High contradictorily foreclosed identificatory alternatives for urban households. For example, bell hooks (1990) argues that rather than a space of worthless upheaval, the "homeplace" of African American families are sites of humanization and resistance:

> The task of making homeplace . . . was about the construction of a safe place where black people could affirm one another and by so doing heal many of the wounds inflicted by racist domination. We could not learn to love or respect ourselves in the culture of white supremacy, on the outside; it was there on the inside, in that "homeplace" that we had the opportunity to grow and develop, to nurture our spirits (p. 42).

Urban homes and neighborhoods have served as spaces for the development of networks of survival, social organization, and the cultivation of cultural and political identities (hooks, 1990; Haymes, 1995). This understanding that the urban home may be a "homeplace" of strength, recovery, and positive identity-making is significant. It challenges prevailing narratives of purposeless, unstable, urban neighborhoods.

The discursive practices of teachers and staff constituted schools as places where good things can happen, and opened up new ways to understand the urban school—as a place of community and nurturance. Nonetheless, they problematically recirculated "culture of poverty" storylines of urban households. The irony of these discursive practices raises the question: How might we speak and think in ways that allow for more than dualistic categories such as "good" or "bad?"

"Comeback Kids"

In addition to constructing urban student identities as victims of urban warfare, teachers and staff also testified to the strength of their students. The students at Dynamic were positioned as strong or resilient in two primary ways. First, students are strong because they are positive and able to endure the hardships of their daily lives. Ms. Perry, for example, shared:

> *Ms. Perry:* Their eating is not always consistent. And nutrition can undermine their health; their health can undermine their ability to study. Depression, I'm sure, is one of the most undiagnosed realities that people in poverty struggle with. And I know that a lot of our kids' parents are depressed or are dealing with losing their jobs and alcoholism and so on. Do these things happen in more affluent populations? Yes. But I think statistically the frequency of them happening here might be greater: the numbers, the critical mass of them. And yet I still think our kids are incredible. I think there's an amazing resiliency of energy here. And I think our students—on the whole my perception of the students—is that they are impressively positive. They're *impressively determined to survive* (my emphasis).

Like other teachers, Ms. Perry noted the range of health and social issues that may impact the ability of students to learn in school. Her remarks about depression and alcoholism as being part of the struggle of people living in poverty reiterate narratives of embattled urban homes and neighborhoods. The comment that students are "impressively determined to survive" suggests a marveling at their ability to simply wake up each morning and continue to exist.

Second, Dynamic students were positioned as strong for their ability to attain high academic success despite their social, cultural,

economic, and political marginalization. Here, daily life experiences
of poverty, gang involvement, domestic violence, and homelessness
are juxtaposed with accounts of extraordinary success. Consider, for
example, Mr. Sullivan's remarks:

> *Mr. Sullivan:* We are the only high school in the city to receive
> Title I funding. We're at 70% poverty. Three out of every
> four students that we see in this building live in poverty.
> Having said that, you can obviously infer that we have many
> of the *same problems that classic inner-city schools have, whether
> it be gangs, whether it be domestic violence, homeless kids.* I mean,
> we've got all of that stuff. I know *one of my kids right now
> that's married and living out of a car with her husband.* And so I
> mean, that's there. And that's sort of omnipresent. I mean,
> it's so much everywhere that I think sometimes you almost
> see past it. Because it's kind of like when you live out in
> the mountains you don't look at them anymore (laughs),
> you take them for granted. And here, I think sometimes
> we have a tendency to do that as well. *Because there are a lot
> of kids that are resilient.* I mean, look at the Open Program[1]
> which I'm the coordinator of and 78% of the kids live in
> poverty. A couple of my kids, two of them in particular, are
> very outstanding students, I mean, 3.8, 3.9 GPA—outstand-
> ing workers. *I know one of them lives in abject poverty. And he's
> going to be going to [a small, elite liberal arts college]. He got a
> scholarship there* (my emphasis).

According to Mr. Sullivan, the manifestation of urban problems at
Dynamic is so pervasive that it is "omnipresent" or "so much everywhere."
Issues of domestic abuse and poverty are so normal that "it's kind of like
when you live out in the mountains you don't look at them anymore,
you take them for granted." The emphasis on the omnipresence of
urban problems at one level testifies to the longevity and persistence
of poverty. But at another level, it insidiously naturalizes issues such
as gang activity, homelessness, and abuse as an intrinsic characteristic
of urban life and identities.

Even in the midst of the normative challenges of urban life,
Mr. Sullivan tells us that, "a lot of kids [are] resilient." In the case of
some students, their strength and perseverance have allowed them to
overcome situations of "abject poverty" to become scholarship winners.
Behind these observations lurk storylines of "comeback kids" (see,
e.g., Tillotson, 1994) or of students who "beat the odds and will soon

be·off to college" (Brandt, 2007, p. 1B). Stories about urban students "beating the odds" deploy a variety of messages. Most transparently, success stories attest to the power of hard work and determination. When Mr. Sullivan shared that one of his students received a scholarship to an elite college, he was also validating the importance of students being "outstanding workers." In this account, I not only heard a story about the students at Dynamic High, but additionally, I heard the plotlines of Horatio Alger's stories, echoes of Abraham Lincoln's log cabin-to-White House narrative, and the beginning utterances of a story about upward mobility. Mr. Sullivan's narrative of the strength and achievements of students entwined with ideas about meritocracy and the importance of a good work ethic. Paradoxically, storylines of perseverance and "beat the odds" success also highlight and redeploy messages about the destitution of urban life. Accounts of resilience end up contributing to and strengthening metaphors of "war babies" and "war zones" to describe the experiences of urban students and residents.

Recall the "easy" story I told in Chapter 1 about Trina. As an easy story, it was a version of the "beating the odds" accounts of teachers and staff at Dynamic High. To a degree, my story was different from the stories of teachers and staff that discursively frame urban neighborhoods as "war zones" of "instability." Yet, while it did not position urban students such as Trina as "war babies," it shared a fundamental characteristic with discourses of urban dysfunction. The complexity and incongruity of urban, immigrant experiences are smoothed out and reduced to simplistic narratives of perseverance and "comeback kid" triumph. Albeit a positive portrayal, the attempt to illuminate the difficulties faced by poor urban and other minoritized populations through storylines of resilience nonetheless contributes to the problematic essentialization of their experiences. The identities and experiences of urban students and families are simplified into dualisms of "resistant," "resilient," and "strong" *or* "oppressed," "victimized," and "mistreated" (Fine & Weis, 1998; Lubienski, 2003).

Writing about the predominance of binary stories that underscore problems and victimization on one hand, and strength and triumph on the other, Fine and Weis (1998) explain:

> Simple stories of discrimination and victimization, with no evidence of resistance, resilience, or agency, are seriously flawed, deceptively partial, and they deny the rich subjectivities of persons surviving amidst horrific social circumstances. Equally dreary, however, are the increasingly popular stories

of individual heroes who thrive despite, denying the burdens
of surviving amidst such circumstances (p. 286).

For Fine and Weis, there are two prevailing types of "simple stories"
about urban residents. One common plotline depicts urban residents
as helpless victims, overcome by the power of their oppressors. In its
simplicity, this narrative discounts acts of contestation and dissent.
The second storyline privileges themes of "success," "resilience," and
"agency." Urban students, for example, are portrayed as "comeback
kids" who are able to rise above their oppression and succeed. These
feel-good stories are also problematic because they divert attention
from systemic practices that create and perpetuate unequal educational
practices and outcomes (Anyon 1997; Kozol 1991). Ironically, both of
the storylines reinscribe and further marginalize those who are different and "Other" and maintain the hegemony of binary categories of
us/them and normal/not normal.

The framing of urban students as "war babies" and "comeback
kids" and the urban school as "shelter" are in different ways smooth,
"easy" stories. These one-dimensional storylines leave out details and
jagged edges that speak to complicated, unresolved identities. As I turn
to a closer examination of the identity work of Lao American students
in Chapter 4, I begin to explore the ways dominant discourses shape
their experiences and identities at Dynamic High School. I elucidate
the ways our simplistic stories confine the identities of urban, Lao
students and mask the conflicts and uncertainties that occur in the
double movement of identity.

4

Confining Immigrant Identities

Culture is conceived along ethnically absolute lines, not as something intrinsically fluid, changing, unstable and dynamic, but as a fixed property of social groups rather than a relation field in which they encounter one another and live out social, historical relationships. When culture is brought into contact with race it is transformed into a pseudobiological property of communal life.

—Paul Gilroy, *There Ain't no Black in the Union Jack*

A couple of years after I graduated from college, I was walking with three friends on the campus of the University of Minnesota. Although none of us were connected to the University, we were there to enjoy the sunshine of the summer day. As we slowly strolled down the sidewalk of a street with various shops and restaurants, we walked past a group of three men seated on top of a picnic table. When we were a few feet from the men, one of them laughingly remarked, "Look at that Chink with the gringos." Without pause, my friends and I continued to walk for another 20 feet. At this point, I suddenly realized that the name-calling of "Chink" was directed at me. Immediately, I whipped around and yelled, "I'm not Chinese!" The three men looked at me in shock, not expecting such a vehement delayed response. My friends, two White American women and one White American man, mirrored the men's surprise. As we continued to walk again, I explained unnecessarily to my friends (who already knew my ethnic background) that my heritage is Vietnamese and not Chinese.

My positioning as "Chinese" in this and myriad other instances in my life is part of a larger set of discursive practices that tell a certain story about the static, harmonious, unity of Asian immigrant identities. The dominance of discourses that position Asian Americans as perpetual foreigners and model minorities has prompted scholars such as Mia Tuan (1998) to ask if we will be "Forever foreigners or honorary whites?" In the double movement of identity, as we draw on discourses to make meaning for ourselves, others also use discourses that are available to understand or identify us. For instance, as a person of Vietnamese heritage who has lived in the United States for most of my life, I might identify myself as an Asian American. However, others may identify me as Chinese because my physical appearance matches with a history of ideas and images of what they know about people of Chinese descent. The (mist)taking of my identity as Chinese by the three men, then, is a problem of history and old ideas of what it means to be a person of Asian descent.

Bronwyn Davies (2000) tells us that "the means for moving beyond the old ways of thinking and speaking [about identity lies] with the analysis of how existing discursive practices trap us into the worlds we are trying to move beyond" (p. 38). In this chapter, I take up this suggestion by explicating the double movement of Lao student identities within the discursive space of schooling (Yon, 2000) at Dynamic High. I illustrate the ways existing discursive practices about ethnic and racial identity place students in restrictive, simplistic subject positions. I then explore the tensions and complications that arise as students attempt to "move beyond" and stake out subject positions for themselves.

Positioning Lao American Students

"People Call Asian People Just Chinese"

One way to think about the way dominant discourses work is to think about the stereotypes or myths that exist and are circulated about different immigrant groups. For immigrants in general, these dominant discourses or stereotypes include the perception that immigrants are a burden on the U.S. economy and take jobs from "real" Americans (Lowe, 1996; Tuan, 1998). According to Robert Lee (1999) discourses that have portrayed Asian immigrants as alien and foreign include 6 images: the pollutant, the coolie, the deviant, the yellow peril, the model minority, and the gook. Contemporary, pervasive stereotypes include the perception that Asian immigrants are all computer geniuses, good at math, passive and quiet, or are martial arts experts (Lee, 1996). An important characteristic of dominant discourses is that they lump or categorize individuals into one-dimensional, generalizing categories that ignore the nuances, inconsistencies, and instabilities of identity. This process of classification, according to Davies (2000), is "dangerous" because it "can be a way of controlling, of reducing, of slotting someone into that which is already known" (p. 38). For individuals of Asian descent, their classification often reduces the multiplicity of their ethnic backgrounds into "known" categories such as "Chinese" or "Japanese" (Lee, 1999; Pang, 1990). At best, this process masks the diversity of Asian groups, including those of Cambodian, Chinese, East Indian, Filipino, Guamanian, Hawaiian, Hmong, Indonesian, Japanese, Korean, Lao, Samoan, Taiwanese, and Vietnamese heritages, among others (Pang, 1990).[1] At worst, and as this chapter reveals, it creates the marginalization and misrecognition of identities.

At Dynamic High, where nearly half (38%) of the students were Asian American, the process of classification positioned all Asian students as "the same" (Lee, 1996), where all students of Asian descent were categorized under 3 labels: "Asian," "Hmong," and "Chinese." Elucidating this discursive practice, Chintana, one of the Lao American students, shared:

> *Chintana*: A lot of people call Asian people just Chinese or something. I hear it all the time. . . . I've heard it like, they'll say "That Chinese boy." And I'm sitting here thinking, "He's not Chinese." 'Cause I can tell the difference almost all the time.

> *BN*: They don't say he's Hmong or they're all Hmong?

> *Chintana*: No. Some of them say it, because then most of them think that everybody here is Hmong. But most of them think it's like Chinese or something (laughs).

Regardless of ethnic background, students and teachers "call Asian people just Chinese." This occurred even though most of the students knew that the majority of the students at the school were Hmong. As an Asian student of Lao ethnic heritage, Chintana noted that she "can tell the difference almost all the time." The discursive location of all Asian immigrants within homogenizing categories of "Asian," "Hmong," and "Chinese" ignores the variation in what it means to be an Asian ethnic in the United States. While dominant discourses mask critical differences related to ethnic (and economic, religious, and educational) backgrounds, as we see later in the chapter, the distinctions of ethnic identity matter a great deal to Lao American students at the school.

The discursive positioning of Asian immigrant students as "Chinese" exemplifies the central role of discourses in how we make sense of identity. In the case of the Asian American students at the school, the narratives that circulate in popular culture contribute significantly to how they made sense of what it means to be an Asian ethnic. Consider Ms. Anderson's observation about Jackie Chan:

> *Ms. Anderson:* I think that 'cause there are not that many Lao students anymore at this school, they tend to get lumped in with Asian kids. . . . I think, from the student perspective I don't think most of the students—Okay, students who are Hmong obviously know that the Lao kids are Lao. And other Asian kids know. But I think that as far as, if you look at the African kids, they have no idea. No idea who's Hmong and who's Lao and who's Chinese. I mean I've had a lot of the kids in my 6th hour who refer to all Hmong as Chinese. And Jackie Chan is their sort of national hero.

Similar to Chintana, Ms. Anderson believed that "other Asian kids know" about ethnic distinctions between the students and recognize "who's Hmong and who's Lao and who's Chinese." In contrast, non-Asian students such as African (e.g., Liberian, Oromo) students "have no idea." According to Ms. Anderson, the overwhelming perception of Hmong students is that they are Chinese and that "Jackie Chan is their sort of national hero." As a cultural icon, the Chinese actor Jackie Chan is known for his martial arts and action movies. Students at Dynamic drew on these available discourses about what it means to be Asian to position Hmong and other Asian American students at the school as "Chinese."

The discursive positioning of Lao students as "[j]ust another Chinese kid" and the way that students and staff "lump all Asians as Chinese" was viewed as particularly reprehensible by Ms. Kane:

> *Ms. Kane:* And if you say, *"No we don't have, we only have one Chinese in this building,"* then they say, *"Oh, I mean Japanese."* So they don't seem to see that [there are] Koreans, and Asians, [and] Malaysians and there are these differences. I wanted to add one thing about how our Laotians are perceived. I think by support staff they see no difference. They don't even have a consciousness. . . . I think a lot of teachers just say, "Oh, those are the Hmong kids with the Lao name, with the long names." And they don't see a difference. They don't know it's different. They don't even know it's a different language, let alone a kind of a different culture and then even farther down, of course *no concept at all of the past history of the relationship between Hmong and Lao.* So

I think *a lot of teachers just think of them as Hmong with long
names* (my emphasis).

The response of "Oh, I mean Japanese" to Ms. Kane's correction that
the Asian students at Dynamic were not Chinese hails another dominant understanding of Asian ethnics—as Japanese.[2] As Ms. Kane points
out, individuals of Asian heritage have different histories, cultures, and
languages. Problematically, the categorization of all Asian ethnic groups
into one-dimensional categories ignores longstanding tensions between
some groups, such as the Lao and Hmong in Laos. Teachers and staff
have "no concept at all of the past history of the relationship between
Hmong and Lao" and "don't even have a consciousness" of the differences between students. As Ms. Kane criticized, "a lot of teachers just
think of [Lao students] as Hmong with long names." Indeed, other
teachers admitted to this transgression. Mr. Sullivan, for example, dis-
closed: "I doubt that most staff even acknowledge that kids are Lao.
In fact, the only real indicator of being Lao is a name that is like 30
letters long." Other teachers were also contrite about their simplistic
positioning of Lao students. Ms. Jenkins, for example, confessed, "And
that's something that I need to work on too, just learning more about
instead of just kind of clumping all my Asian students together. Because
they're very different and they have different backgrounds, cultures,
and expectations."

The implication of the identification of Lao American students
within discrete categories such as "Hmong" or "Chinese" is that whether
or not Lao students wanted to identify as "Lao American," "Asian,"
"American"—or all of these categories and more—were foreclosed to
the students. For racialized ethnics such as Lao American students,
this predicament of identity is perhaps more complicated, because
they have both a racial identity (i.e., as Asian) and an ethnic identity
(i.e., as Lao). The definitions of race and ethnicity put forward by
Mittelberg and Waters (1992) are helpful here:

> [R]ace has been used by theorists to refer to distinctions
> drawn from physical appearance. Ethnicity has been used to
> refer to the distinctions based on national origin, language,
> religion, food—and other cultural markers (p. 425).

This distinction between race and ethnicity is important for understanding the multiple, fragmented process of identification. At Dynamic
High, while Lao American students may choose to claim an ethnic
identity as Lao, they may be constituted by others in terms of their

racial identity as Asian (Tuan, 1998). Or, we can also imagine that students may prefer a national identity as "American" but be placed in subject positions that emphasize an ethnic identity (i.e., Lao) or a racial identity (i.e., Asian).

In the experience of racialized ethnics, Tuan (1998) suggests that "their racial and ethnic identities crosscut and compete with each other for dominance, with race almost always overriding ethnicity" (p. 22). I would extend Tuan's analysis by suggesting that our discourses have problematically privileged race over ethnicity. For example, within the discourse on race in the United States, the experiences of minority groups are understood exclusively within the racial framework of Black/White relations. As Hune (2000) cogently argues, "[a]ll power and race relations have come to be seen within this framework of subordinate/majority dynamics" (p. 668). At Dynamic High School, where Asian American students included individuals from multiple Asian ethnic groups, ethnicity and race were both salient factors in the experiences of Lao American students. However, as we see in this chapter, the emphasis on Black/White racial relations and subordinate/majority dynamics obscures the interethnic tensions (i.e., between Lao American and Hmong American students) and intraethnic tensions (i.e., among Lao American students) of identity work.

Yet, and more complicated, the misrecognition of Asian American identities cannot be resolved, as Ms. Kane and Ms. Jenkins suggested above, through learning about the different backgrounds, histories, and cultures of Asian ethnic groups. As the next section demonstrates, such an understanding of identity is grounded in originary notions of culture and identity (Bhabha, 1994), and thus fails to account for the flux, contradictions, and temporariness of identity.

"Celebrating" Asian Identities

The positioning of Lao American students within essentialist discourses that framed them as "Chinese"—or at best "Hmong"—exists within a larger web of power relations that have long marginalized the histories and identities of Asian Americans (and other groups) in the United States. The attempt to remedy the exclusion of different groups and experiences has manifested most frequently within the overarching philosophy of "multiculturalism." As a political philosophy of "many cultures" (Ladson-Billings & Tate, 1995) multiculturalism is a response to what Goldberg (1994) calls the "monoculturalism as intellectual ideology and institutional practice" of "Eurovision" (p. 5). Multiculturalism in schools, most commonly known as "multicultural education" (Banks, 1995; Bennett,

2001), often attempts to heal the past wounds of violence and exclusion. It is marked by efforts that emphasize "inclusion," "celebration," and "affirmation" of the knowledges, experiences, cultures, and identities of historically marginalized groups (Banks, 1995; Mohanty, 1994).

At Dynamic High celebrating the identities and achievements of a group is perhaps best exemplified by the activities of the Asian Cultural Club, also known as the "Asian Club" to students and staff. As Mr. Her, the Asian Club advisor and Hmong bilingual teacher, explained to me, the Club had two primary purposes. First, it offered Asian American students a place to fit in at the school. Addressing the issue of belonging was critical, because when Mr. Her arrived at the school the Asian American students were "outcast" in the school community. The Club changed this by fostering among Asian American students a feeling and space for belonging, ownership, and insider-ship. It accomplished this, according to Mr. Her, by instilling cultural pride and cultural awareness through Club activities. Second, the Asian Club served the purpose of providing students with leadership opportunities. In the Asian Club, "If you're good at something you can shine. You can bring it to the group. You can show them and exercise some leadership." Additionally, as Mr. Her pointed out to nearly 100 students at the first Club meeting, taking leadership positions will give the students important "experience for resumes and college applications."

The goals of the Asian Club played out in a variety of activities that the Club organized for the student body throughout the year, including a dance in the winter and one in the spring as well as a dinner for Asian American parents. Of these activities, perhaps the largest and most visible event was the "Asian Show." This event took place during Asian American Month in May and featured fashion, music, and dance. In a memo to faculty and staff, Mr. Her referred to the show as the "Asian Cultural Club Assembly" and explained: "The purpose of this year's program is [to] use musical performance to show cultural transitions Asian teenagers have undergone—from traditional to modern."

Each of the shows featured eight acts, and the acts were different for each show. The acts combined clothes fashion with dance and music. According to Mr. Her's memo, the acts transitioned from more "traditional" clothes, music, and dance to more "contemporary" clothes, music, and dance. For example, in the beginning the performers were dressed in "traditional" costumes and lip-synched and danced to music that was in Hmong or Lao. By the end of the show, the "modern" performances included a heavy metal band as well as English-language hip-hop songs, dance moves, and clothes.

The students and staff who attended the shows cheered and applauded enthusiastically throughout both of the shows. Students stood up and danced to the music and sang along with songs that were in English as well as in Lao or Hmong. At one point, when three Hmong girls came out in Lao woven-silk dresses and danced to a Lao song, one of the Lao American students sitting next to me raised and extended his arm in support. As he moved his arm to the left and right to the beat of the music, the student said "Heeey." Indeed, the atmosphere was close to disorder. Teachers standing at the perimeter, on the outside aisles, were alert for signs of trouble. The darkness of the auditorium and loud beats of the music combined with the shouts and liveliness of the students to create a heady atmosphere. As I sat watching students shed classroom decorum for laughter, cheers and gyrations, I realized that the physical, vocal, and emotional responses the Show evoked in students were similar to those in pep rallies or pop music concerts.

At the end of the Show, Toua, a Hmong student who was the vice president of the Asian Club came onto the stage amidst loud applause. After taking a moment to quiet the students, he closed the Show by reading from a prepared script:

> *Toua:* Hey so *how you guys enjoy this Asian fantasy?* I hope you guys was [sic] touch and left with a piece of memory embedded in your heart of the touch of Asianicity. My name is Toua Yang, I am the vice president of Asian Club. There's been a lot of confusion with the Asian Club.[3] *The purpose of this Asian Club is to educate and teach others about the Asian culture. The world suffers with discrimination because the world lacks knowledge of other cultures.* We the Asian Club is trying to make a difference starting with teaching our school, the best school ever, Dynamic High School. Thankx[4] (my emphasis).

From Toua's perspective, the purpose of the Show was to teach students and staff about the culture and experiences of Asian Americans—or as he put it, a "touch of Asianicity." This "Asian fantasy" approach to addressing issues of cultural difference was couched in terms of a need to "educate and teach others about the Asian culture" because the "world suffers with discrimination because the world lacks knowledge of other cultures." This view that the role of the Asian Club is to combat inequality by providing students with "knowledge of other cultures" resonates with the social justice and reform goals of multicultural education (see, e.g., Banks, 1995; Sheets, 2003). The Asian Show's attempt to teach the customs, aesthetics, and languages of Asian students through music and dance as a way to address discrimination and marginalization was consistent with dominant practices of multicultural education.

Paradoxically, in the double movement of identity, the response of Asian American students (i.e., Asian Club members) to their construction as "Other" reinscribed the essentialist identities that they sought to combat. The showcase of clothes, music, and dance from different Asian ethnic groups—albeit an attempt to illustrate cultural transitions—made claims to some sort of "authentic" or "real" culture or identity. In doing so, the Show simultaneously reinforced Orientalist discourses (Said, 1979) of an essential identity and exoticized (Clifford, 1988) what it means to be Asian American. Indeed, Toua's question, "[H]ow you guys enjoy this Asian fantasy?" redeployed notions of the "Asian mystique" (Prasso, 2005; Said, 1979) exemplified by the subjectification of Asian women as hypersexual "Geisha girls" and "China dolls" (Lee, 1999; Prasso, 2005).

The contradictory effect of "inclusive" multiculturalism is that inclusion and exclusion—or the production of margin and center—became part of the same process (Gitlin, Buendia, Crosland & Doumbia, 2003). The emphasis on the difference of groups reinscribed their position as "Other." Put another way, Britzman (1998) asks us to consider, "How different can these different folks be and still be recognized as just like everyone else" (p. 86)? Mr. Her and Asian Club students such as Toua were part of the process that reconstituted the boundaries of "normal," and defined them as different and "not normal." While they wanted the Asian Show to demonstrate *changes* in the cultures of Asian students, it instead reified their identities and experiences. Likewise, even though students like Toua may want to critically address discrimination, the Asian Show reduced oppressive experiences to song and dance. The theatrical "performance" of the Asian Show in effect was a "performance" of identity (Butler, 1993) that resignified "the originary binary opposition of 'us/them' in more elaborate and normalizing terms" (Britzman, 1998, p. 88).

The Struggle to Be Known

"I'm Kind of Special, Don't You Know"

As a site of struggle against the essentializing norms of discourses about Asian American identities at Dynamic High, the Asian Show and the Asian Club were not free of the contradictions of identity work. Rather than a simple space where all Asian American students could univocally respond to broader oppressive discourses that marginalized their identities and experiences, the Asian Show and Asian Club were themselves sites of conflict and contestation between Hmong American and Lao American students (among other Asian ethnics). The sanctioned school activities of the Asian Club and Asian Show privileged the identities of Hmong students and simultaneously maintained and exacerbated the alienation of Lao students.

This fractured outcome is the result of a complex, nonlinear process of identification that complicates our notions of pedagogical intentions (Ellsworth, 1997). Although the Asian Club was intended to be a space that nurtured the identities of Asian American students by offering a space where they could belong, Lao students did not participate. Essentializing discourses that framed the identities of Lao students as "Hmong" or "Chinese" combined with the statistical majority of Hmong students at the school to create an unwelcoming environment for Lao students. Lao students (and other non-Asian students) pointedly called the Asian Club the "Hmong Club," and did not participate in Club or Asian Show activities because they were not really "Asian" but "Hmong." Ms. Kane noted the absence of Lao and other non-Hmong Asian students in this way:

> *Ms. Kane*: Asian Club is having Parent Night. Asian Club had a show. Okay, I didn't see Lao kids there. I didn't see Chinese, I didn't see Hmong, I mean, I saw Hmong. I didn't see a Korean. I didn't see Indian. I didn't see people from these other cultures, Southeast Asian cultures that we have in our building and yet they weren't part of it.

As Ms. Kane made sense of why other "Southeast Asian cultures . . . in our building . . . weren't part of [the Asian Show]," she attributed it to the fact that "they're not asked or the kids in Asian Club are all Hmong." On the level of practice, Ms. Kane pointed to institutional practices of exclusion, where invitations to events such as Asian Parent Night were only translated from English to Hmong and not other Asian languages: "When it's announced they'll be saying, 'Asian Parent Night,' and none of my kids received a notice in anything other than English or Hmong. . . . There was no translation handed out in Lao, in Thai, in any of the other Asian languages."

Indeed, in his closing speech, when Toua commented that, "There's been a lot of confusion with the Asian Club," he was alluding to the discontent circulating among non-Hmong students who were unhappy about the purpose of the Club and the lack of non-Hmong Asian students in its leadership and membership. Within the precarious, contested space of identity, the attempts of the Asian Show to combat discrimination faced by Asian Americans, paradoxically became a site of the exclusion of Lao and other Asian ethnic groups at the school. An implication of the cultural politics of identity that homogenized the experiences of all Asian ethnic groups at Dynamic was the masking of historical and continuing tensions between various Asian ethnic groups. Consider, for instance, the remarks that Sompong made during lunch one day:

> *I share with the students some of the comments that students in Ms. Hanson's class made about racism and ask them if they think there's racism at Dynamic. Sompong and Kia say no, and point out there's a lot of "mixture" or diversity at the school. They tell me that different kinds of students hang out together and are friends. They point to our table as an example, where Lao, Hmong, and White students sit together. After a little thought, however, Sompong declares that if there's a racist group at the school, it is the Hmong. She quickly touches Kia [a Hmong student] on the arm and apologizes to her, and states that she doesn't mean to disrespect any specific person. She continues to explain that many of the Hmong students sit together and hang out exclusively with other Hmong students. Sompong then pauses and gestures at the Hmong students sitting together at the tables around us and our eyes scan the cafeteria with her. Continuing, she turns to me and asserts that many of the Hmong students "hate on me because I'm Laos." Once again, Sompong remembers that Kia and Bao are Hmong and qualifies her remark by adding, "Not all Hmong people are that way"* (FN 2/6/02, 3rd Lunch).

According to Sompong, the Hmong students at Dynamic are "racist" because they group together and exclude students from other ethnic and racial groups. Although she mistakes the ethnic tensions with Hmong students as "racism," her perspective reveals the marginalization of ethnicity as a site of conflict. As Sompong put it, "[Hmong students] hate on me because I'm Laos." However, the privileging of race and race relations in our dominant discourses obscures this complex wrangling of identity, and as we saw, even exacerbates the problem through multicultural discourses of "inclusion."

The failure of teachers and other students to recognize the distinctiveness of ethnic and individual identities was of particular note to the Lao students. Their exclusion and misrecognition at Dynamic garnered indictments by Lao students such as Mindy: "They know more about the Hmong students than the Lao students." The marginalization of Lao students was also evident to some teachers. Ms. Perry, for example, observed that the misrecognition of Lao students played out in various ways at the school:

> *Ms. Perry:* Sometimes I perceive Laotian students as feeling marginalized in the classroom, either by me, the teacher, not saying Laotian as often as I say Hmong. Or sometimes I see a little bit of hesitancy or separation—prejudice actually, from some of the Hmong males towards some of the Laotian males at different times, or teasing, or taunting.

At Dynamic, the exclusion of Lao students may occur through the failure of teachers to acknowledge their ethnic identity, or through acts of "hesitancy," "separation," and "prejudice" by Hmong students. For Ms. Kane, the desires and claims of identity were a struggle by Lao (and other Asian ethnic) students to be known:

> *Ms. Kane:* People lump them together you know. And they do have a little separation from other Southeast Asians as all do. The Chinese kids want to be known as Chinese, and the Hmong want to be known, "I'm Hmong; I'm not Chinese," and the Lao kids, "I'm Lao; I'm not Thai. *I'm kind of special, don't you know.* I can speak Lao language" (my emphasis).

Lao American students at Dynamic High School faced multiple, interconnecting dilemmas in their identity work. On one hand, they struggled against racializing (Omi and Winant 1994; Tuan 1998) practices that essentialized and marginalized their identities and experiences. On the other hand, they struggled against their peers, teachers and parents to be known as unique individuals. The positioning of Lao American students as "Chinese" or "Hmong" effectively ignored identity claims that, "I'm kind of special, don't you know."

The Double Movement of Identity

Recall that in the double movement of identity, our identities are not exclusively determined by the dominant discourses of other people. Because culture and identity are shaped within social relationships (Davies, 2000; Hall, 1996), the work of identity construction is fraught with tensions and disagreements. At the same time as others take up certain discourses to identify us, we also draw on discourses to make meaning for ourselves. This process opens up room for multiple, contradictory positionings as we identify or do not identify with the subject positions to which we are summoned. Put another way, expectations from others of *who we are or should be* may collide and conflict with *how we want to identify ourselves*. This process of negotiation and struggle, where we are recognized or misrecognized as the identities that we take up, is the predicament of Lao American students at Dynamic High. Charles Taylor (1994) refers to identity struggles between what we want to take up personally as individuals and the ways we are understood publically as "the politics of recognition" p. (81). As he explains:

> [O]ur identity is partly shaped by recognition or its absence, often by the misrecognition of others, and so a person or group of people can suffer real damage, real distortion, if the people or society around them mirror back to them a confining or demeaning, or contemptible picture of themselves. Nonrecognition or misrecognition can inflict harm, can be a form of oppression, imprisoning someone in a false, distorted, and reduced mode of being (Taylor, 1994, p. 74).

Because the discourses through which we are constituted are multiple, partial, and contradictory, opportunities open up for misrecognition. As we saw in the experiences of Lao students at Dynamic High, their identities were misrecognized as "Hmong," "Chinese," and "Other." Such misrecognition, according to Taylor, may "inflict harm, can be a form of oppression, imprisoning someone in a false, distorted and reduced mode of being."

For Lao American students, the misrecognition of identity did not occur only through the essentialization and racialization of their identity as "Asian" or through the (mis)taking of their ethnic identity as "Chinese" and "Hmong." Further, because identity work is multiply located and incongruous, the ethnic identity of the Lao students was a site of contestation. In the following, I share the identity negotiations of two Lao students, Lori and Mindy, and their struggles with the ways peers and parents "mirror[ed] back to them a confining or demeaning, or contemptible picture of themselves" (Taylor, 1994, p. 74). I pay particular attention to the interethnic tensions of identity work between Lao and Hmong students; as well as the intraethnic tensions between Lao students and their Lao peers and parents.

LORI

For Lao American students at Dynamic High School, being "Lao" was a
site of conflict and misrecognition in various ways. The sheer number
of Hmong students played a major role in the misrecognition of their
Lao identity. This not only occurred at the wider level of the school
as we saw—where all Asian ethnics were essentialized as "Hmong" or
"Chinese"—but also in the interpersonal relations between Lao students
and Hmong students. In Lori's experience, being "Lao" was a particular point of conflict between her and the Hmong female students at
Dynamic. In our conversations, she shared the ways in which her identity was mirrored back in a demeaning way (Taylor, 1994) by Hmong
students who judged and disciplined her with their gaze (Foucault,
1979). As she shared: "[I]f you walk past them they just look at you
mean or judge you by just looking at you. You can tell when people
are judging you with their eyes or something." As Lori elaborated on
the tensions she experienced, she talked about her sense of the false
friendships that she had with the Hmong American girls:

> *Lori*: It's mostly if you have friends that are Hmong and
> they don't really hang with you or something. Like they
> have their own, if you're in the same classroom with them,
> you have two classrooms with them. You guys are friends
> in that classroom where they don't have any of their other
> Hmong friends. And then if you go to another classroom
> and you guys are in the same classroom and they have
> their other Hmong friends. They probably split out with
> you and *just go and stick with Hmong friends instead of you.*
> That's kind of another thing I don't like about some of
> them (my emphasis).

While teachers and non-Asian students may lump all Asian American
students together, ethnic differences do matter for Lao and Hmong
students at Dynamic. As a Lao student at a school predominated by
Hmong students, Lori's experiences told her that Hmong students
only wanted to be friends with her when their Hmong friends were
not present. Otherwise, because she was Lao and not Hmong, the
Hmong girls would "just go and stick with Hmong friends instead of
you." Her Lao identity was constituted as an "Other" who was not the
first choice in friendship. Speaking of the fluctuating friendships with
Hmong girls, Lori remarked, "That's kind of another thing I don't
like about some of them."

The problem of being "Lao" for Lori was more than a problem
of the everyday tensions that inhere in adolescent friendships. Her

identity as Lao American produced material consequences of harm and confinement (Taylor, 1994) that affected her decisions to participate in extracurricular activities at school.

> *Lori*: I would [participate in extracurricular activities] if I had a friend or someone I knew very well in like the Asian Club. Well I know there's some people in the Asian Culture Club, but it's kind of hard. It's more easier for me to have my own race [sic] I guess to be with me. Like if it was for the Asian Culture Club, for the Laotians students to be in there with me. Like Nikhong, if she was going then it would be easier for me to be in it. But if I was the only person it's hard for me, 'cause I'm not good with communicating with Hmong and other race [sic]. It's hard.

Rendered different and "Other" at the school through the disciplinary gaze of Hmong students, Lori was conscious of her difference. She did not feel comfortable participating in the Asian Club or other extracurricular activities at school without the presence of other Lao students. The physically constraining force of power (Othering) is passed over to the very students who are to be subjected by it (Foucault, 1979). At Dynamic High, students like Lori "inscribe[d] in [themselves] the power relation in which [they] simultaneously play[ed] both roles of oppressor and oppressed"—becoming the principle of their own subjection (Foucault, 1979, p. 202).

In addition to limiting physical activities, Lori's identity also affected the quantity and quality of her social interactions at Dynamic. As she explained, it was difficult "trying to talk to" or become friends with Hmong girls: "[T]hey already have a group of friends. You're trying to talk to them or something. They wouldn't really be interested in talking to you since they have friends already. So, yeah, I think that's why it's kind of hard to talk to Hmong girls." As she explained how her Lao identity affected her school experiences, she surmised:

> *Lori*: If I was Hmong maybe I'd probably have more friends. Yeah, basically more Hmong friends. Or if I was Black I'd probably have mostly Black friends. But I guess the only difference is that there's not a lot of Lao students. . . . What I see is that there's a lot of Hmong people and they're more friends in a group and stuff instead of diverse.

Being "Lao" for Lori was a barrier to having more friends due to the predominance of Hmong American and African American and the fact "that there's not a lot of Lao students." Alluding to the within-group clustering of students by race and ethnicity, Lori speculated that she would have more friends if she was part of the Hmong majority group at the school. Similarly, she imagined that she would have more African American (Black) friends if she was African American. Instead, because she was (categorized as) Lao, she was excluded through practices where the students were "more friends in a group and stuff instead of diverse."

The ethnic tensions between Lao students like Lori and Hmong female students is especially notable, since her close friends were not just Lao students, but also African American and White American students. Consider my conversation with Lori about the incongruity of her tensions with students who share an Asian identity with her:

> *Lori*: For me, it's more easier to socialize with Black and Whites than Hmong. I don't know why. Yeah, I don't know why (laughs). It's just I can talk to them more. It's kind of weird.
>
> *BN*: They're not Asian. And you would think that the fact that being a Hmong girl and a Laotian girl, you're Asian, there's that bond there that would make it easier.
>
> *Lori*: Yeah, but it's not.
>
> *BN*: But you get along with Black and White girls.
>
> *Lori*: Yeah, yeah. I mean I have classes with lots of Hmong girls and White and Black too. But I don't know why I connect more with White and Black when I have classes with them.

As I tried to make sense of the discursive practices that shaped the social relations between Lori and other students at Dynamic High, I pointed to her shared racial identity with Hmong students as a potential common bond (Espiritu, 1992). Lori's experience that she was able to "connect more with White and Black" students challenges discourses that privilege race as the singular factor in determining the power dynamics of social relations. The everyday identity struggles of Lao students cannot be explicated within majority/minority vertical dynamics or discrete, binary notions of oppressor/oppressed. In the ambivalence of identity, Trinh (1986/1987) reminds us that "there are no social positions exempt from becoming oppressive to others . . . any group—any position—can move into the oppressor role" (p. 6).

MINDY

Yet, ethnic identity is not only a site of struggle between Lao students and other Asian immigrant groups. What it means to be an individual from a particular ethnic group is also unstable and fractured. For Lao students like Mindy, her ethnic identity was part of contested relations between Lao friends and parents. In the case of Mindy, friendships with Hmong students were problematic for her identity as a Lao person. She was accused by Lao American friends and parents of abandoning her identity as a Lao person: ". . . I think my friends are getting mad at me 'cause I'm hanging out with too many Hmong people. . . . I think that they think I'm becoming one of them. I think my parents think that too." Indeed, Mindy's parents asked her, "Why you trying to be like Hmong people, dyeing your hair and stuff like that?" As she elaborated on their concerns, she shared:

> *Mindy:* It's like they think if I hang out with Hmong people I'm going to be bad, right? But to me, I hang out with different kinds of people, and I don't turn out bad. I know what's right and what's wrong sometime.

> *BN:* What are your parents afraid of? When you say they're afraid you're going to turn out bad, what are they afraid of?

> *M:* Like becoming a slut. Like *forgetting your own race [sic].*

> *BN:* What does that mean?

> *M:* Like I would talk American, English at home a lot. They be like *"Don't talk American, you're going to forget your own race [sic], you're going to be American"* and stuff like that (my emphasis).

The response by parents and Lao peers was a (mis)taking—indeed rejection—of Mindy's identity claims. What it meant to be "Lao" for Mindy collided and competed with understandings of being "Lao" for her parents and Lao peers. In the above, Mindy's comments about her struggles provide us with at least two insights into identity work and the double movement of identity. First, taking up a subject position is not just an abstract, theoretical process, but also a physical process (Davies, 1989, p. 14). Being "Lao" required Mindy to take on certain bodily practices and not others. Similar to a boy who would most likely be ridiculed for wearing dresses, Mindy was disciplined by Lao friends and parents for transgressing the physical boundaries of being "Lao." This included the material acts of coloring her hair and hanging out with Hmong students, as well as speaking English at home. Further, Mindy's shift in friendship circles was deemed a shift from a Lao identity to a Hmong identity. As she explained, "I used to hang out with Lao people and stuff. But then I started hanging out with Hmong people. And, I don't know, they just got mad at me." In Mindy's identity work, the failure to conform to the expected characteristics and behaviors of a Lao person resulted in censure.

Second, and in relation, there is a contrastive element to what it means to be "Lao" for Mindy's parents and Lao friends. In the context of Dynamic High and the community surrounding the school, a Lao identity was framed in opposition to a Hmong identity, and to a larger extent, also opposed to an "American" identity. For Lao parents and friends, understanding and distinguishing "me" from "not me" (Davies, 2000, p. 75) was tied up in being "not Hmong." Because Mindy was socializing with Hmong friends and dyeing her hair, they considered her to be "becoming one of them." The disagreement between Mindy and her parents and friends over what it meant to be "Lao" is part of learning what Davies (2000) calls identity "categories."

> We learn categories of people and who is excluded and included in these categories (e.g., male/female, father/daughter). We learn how to participate in the discursive practices that give meaning to those categories, including the storylines in which various positions are elaborated. We learn, more importantly, how to position ourselves in terms of those categories and storylines as though we, in fact, are in one category rather than another (e.g., as girl and not boy, or as "good" girl and not "bad" girl). Finally we come to see ourselves as having those characteristics that locate us in these different categories, as belonging in the world in certain ways and thus seeing it accordingly (p. 44).

As a Lao American student, Mindy was supposed to have learned the category of her Lao membership and "how to participate in the discursive practices that give meaning to [that] categor[y]." Evidently, Mindy failed to learn that part of being "Lao" means taking up physical characteristics and associating with people that are in one category (e.g., Lao) and not in another category (e.g., Hmong). At the same time, because the discursive construction of "me" and "not me" is an unstable, incomplete process, new possibilities for what it means to be an urban, Lao American student opened up. For Mindy, these new possibilities included being able to "hang out with different kinds of people" and dyeing her hair.

The identity work of students like Mindy was messy and pushed outside the limits of coherent categories. Her identity negotiations with parents and Lao peers were infused with a multiplicity of contradictory discourses. For example, the emphasis on her Lao heritage is remarkable because she is the child of a Lao mother and a Vietnamese father. She was born in France and lived there until she was seven years old. Ironically, the central point of conflict between Mindy and her parents and Lao friends was due to actions that blurred their notions of a pure, discrete Lao identity and deployed storylines of a Hmong identity. Indeed, the discursive construction of Mindy's identity as "Lao" is arbitrary and unstable. One could easily argue that she is also "French," "Vietnamese," or simply "American."

Additionally, as Mindy recounted earlier, her parents associated being Hmong with conceptions of "Americanization" that included putting red or blonde streaks in her long black hair and "turn[ing] out bad." Turning out bad included "forgetting your own race" and being sexually promiscuous or "becoming a slut." On one hand, this understanding of Hmong culture and identity echoes popular discourses of Hmong immigrants that emphasize the role of Hmong "traditional" practices in contributing to the high rate of pregnancy and marriage among Hmong teenage girls (Ngo, 2002; Lee, 1997). On the other hand, it contradicts dominant discourses (which we saw in Chapter 1) that frame Hmong culture and identity as rooted in "tradition" (see, e.g., Louwagie & Browning, 2005a, 2005b). However, from the perspective of Mindy's parents, what it means to be Hmong links Hmong culture and identity to the harmful influences of Americanization and practices of Western society rather than notions of tradition. As an exemplar of the way discourses operate to identify individuals, Mindy's case highlights the tendency to regulate identity within simplistic categories.

In the fragmented, ambivalent space of identity a Lao student may consider herself Asian American, her parents may consider her Lao, and non-Lao students may consider her as Chinese or Asian. The double movement of identity opens up a space where conflicts as well as changes are possible. Here, the identities of individuals such as Lori and Mindy may want to claim are not recognized or misrecognized by others because they disrupt ingrained discourses of who they are or should be. For Lori, her ethnic identity as Lao constrained her social relationships and activities at school. In Mindy's case, who she thinks she is and the way she wants to represent herself are at odds with perceptions and expectations of friends and family. The experiences that these Lao American girls had with their parents and friends illuminate the messiness of identity, as well as "what happens when margins generate their own centers" (Chaudhry, 2000, p. 99). As we see further in the next chapter, rather than self-evident and passed from one generation to the next, the cultures and identities of immigrant students are temporary, conflictual, and unresolved.

Unresolved Identities

The new mestiza copes by developing a tolerance for contradictions, a tolerance for ambiguity. She learns to be an Indian in
Mexican culture, to be Mexican from an Anglo point of view.
She learns to juggle cultures. She has a plural personality, she
operates in a pluralistic mode—nothing is thrust out, the good
the bad and the ugly, nothing rejected, nothing abandoned. Not
only does she sustain contradictions, she turns the ambivalence
into something else.

—Gloria Anzaldua, *Borderlands*

Cultural theorist Homi Bhabha suggests that there is a temporal lag
between "the event of the sign" (writing) and "its discursive eventuality
(writing aloud)"—between thought and expression, between intention
to express and verbal performance (Bhabha, 1994). In this ambivalent
space, there is a possibility for modification from the first moment (i.e.,
thought) to the second moment (i.e., verbal expression). For culture
and identity, the space of ambivalence or "Third Space" provides the
possibility for negotiation and change. As Bhabha (1990) elaborates
on the ambivalence of identity or hybridity, he tells us:

> [T]he intervention of hybridity is that it bears the traces
> of those feelings and practices which inform it, just like
> a translation, so that hybridity puts together the traces of
> certain other meanings or discourses . . . [and] gives rise to
> something different, something new and unrecognizable, a
> new area of negotiation and representation (p. 211).

In the ambivalent space of identity there are "incommensurable,"
untranslatable practices or "traces" that linger on in translation. Significantly for Bhabha, identity work involves putting together different
discourses to create something new. More than this, my research suggests

that the ambivalence of identity opens up room for disagreement and confusion.

At Dynamic High the Lao American students were in many ways like the majority of the students at the school. Lao immigrant students listened to music and wore clothes that were inspired by urban, hip-hop aesthetics. Female students usually wore skin-hugging jeans and tight-fitting, knit t-shirts. Male students routinely wore baggy jeans or cargo pants and football jerseys, t-shirts, or un-tucked, button-down shirts. African American, Lao American, Hmong American, Liberian American, and White American students all wore brand label clothes by Gap, Sean John, Nautica, and Tommy Hilfiger. In the corridors and classrooms at Dynamic High, the identities of Lao students as immigrants intersected and blurred with urban, adolescent identities.

And yet, the identity work of Lao American students was not a seamless process, as "identity construction" or "identity negotiation" often imply. As West (2002) points out, "negotiation" suggests that through some sort of genteel conversation, opposing parties are able to come to some sort of final agreement such as a contract. Rather than a point of consensus, the identities of Lao and other immigrant students at Dynamic notably created bewilderment and concern. Ms. Anderson offered these thoughts about the identity work of Lao students:

> *Ms. Anderson:* You look at Tsia in my second hour. He's really on the edge right now. He's in IB, but he's not doing well. . . . Well now he's come back from Spring Break with this new shaved head with the thingy, and wearing blue every single day. There are a lot of kids like who are really having a struggle with their identity. And I think that's true of a lot of the Lao kids as well as some of the Hmong kids. I think it's particularly true in my experience. I think it's particularly true for the kids who came here at a really young age or even some who were born here. . . . That sort of 1.5-generation kids. I think it's really true for a lot of those kids. They're really struggling to find an identity.

Dynamic High teachers such as Ms. Anderson believed that one of the major issues Lao students struggled with included trying to figure out what kind of student or person they wanted to be. As an ELL teacher who taught mostly Lao, Hmong, and Liberian students at the school, Ms. Anderson perceived that "1.5-generation kids" were "really struggling to find an identity." This remark about 1.5-generation immigrant youth importantly alludes to the "between two worlds" discourse. That is, 1.5-generation students are youth who immigrated to the United States when they were still very young. Since these immigrant youth grew up in the United States, their identities are much like those of second-generation immigrants who were born and socialized in U.S. society. However, their identities are unique because they are not quite "Lao" like their first-generation parents and not quite "American" like youth born in the United States.

This understanding of the identity struggles of immigrant students reflects the bicultural model, where identity work is primarily perceived as making a choice between two identities—on one hand, their family's ethnic lineage (as Lao), and on the other their country of residence (as American) (Maira, 2002). While I believe teachers such as Ms. Anderson had deep insights into the experiences of immigrant students, I suggest that the identity work of Lao students extended beyond the "between two worlds" framework. Being "either/or" Americans (Sarroub, 2005) did not seem to be the source of tensions for Lao American students. Rather, for Lao students at Dynamic, the predicament derived primarily from the responses of peers and teachers to their identity claims.

The influence of urban, hip-hop style on Lao male students at the school was especially perplexing for some teachers and students. Ms. Perry talked about the identity work of Lao students in this way:

> *Ms. Perry:* How can I put this? I sometimes sit and observe other classes, and I've watched Laotian males interact with Black males and it's been interesting. Because I don't know if this is racially based or anything, but I mean maybe it's adolescent male, urban adolescent male (laughs). But I see the Laotian male trying to act kind of the gangster-fronting behaviors. And some of the Black males kind of seeing them bewildered by this. And kind of checking each other out, kind of like two dogs of different breeds kind of sniffing and checking each other out. But kind of trying to act the same. . . . It's all an attempt to fit in.

I want to discuss two aspects[1] of this observation of the identity claims of Lao students. First, Ms. Perry characterized the urban, hip-hop style of Lao male students as "gangster-fronting behaviors." Second, she observed that African American students are "bewildered" by Lao male students' style and behaviors.

I suggest that at Dynamic High signs of popular, urban youth culture such as clothes, hairstyles, and music—"gangster-fronting behaviors"—were signified and racialized as African American (Haymes,

1995). Researchers such as Hemmings (2002) have illustrated the ways in which urban high school students integrated "street" style into their identities as urban youth. My research echoes these findings; but also reveals that while the Lao students were incorporating the influences of urban, hip-hop style into their identities as Lao American males, their identity claims were at odds with dominant, racialized images of Asian American men as effeminate (Kumashiro, 1999). Within dominant discourse, Asian American men are supposed to be "quiet Asian boys" (Lei, 2003) instead of tough or "gangster." In the ambivalent space of identity work, Lao male students at Dynamic High were embracing discourses of urban masculinity, "trying to act the same" and aligning themselves with the aesthetics—clothes, music, attitudes—of African American men.

Similar to African American students, many Lao American students sagged their jeans low on their upper thighs to reveal the upper half of their boxer shorts and wore football jerseys and FUBU—ironically the "For Us By Us" clothing brand started by African Americans for African Americans—sweatshirts and jackets. This identity work of Lao students appropriated and translated (Bhabha, 1994) hip-hop culture and created something new, that unsettled hip-hop's relationship with both African American men and Asian American men. According to Bhabha (1990), the "third space" or "ambivalent space" of identity "displaces the histories that constitute it, and sets up new structures of authority, new political initiatives, which are inadequately understood through received wisdom" (p. 211). By displacing the histories that constitute them, Lao students created identities that were in such juxtaposition with dominant "received wisdom" of how they *should* look and act as Asian boys, that it created confusion among other students and teachers.

This response to Lao American male students is also noteworthy because to a large extent all male students at Dynamic High were expected to take up the aesthetics of urban style. As Davidson (1996) notes, high schools are powerful spaces of control where students are expected to conform to "categories of normalcy" dictated by dominant discourses. Similarly, Anderson (1999) argues that the failure of youth to follow the "code of the street" by building "street" reputations resulted in victimization (cf. Flores-Gonzalez, 2005). My research at Dynamic revealed that young men were hassled and called gay if they did not wear pants that were appropriately baggy and sagged to reveal the top half of their boxer shorts (see Ngo, 2003). According to several teachers, students were harassed because they *looked* gay, said the wrong things, wore the wrong clothes, or wore their clothes the wrong way. In a student culture where African American, Asian American, and White American male students appropriated the hip-hop style of African American urban culture, wearing baggy pants and sagging them typified and signified masculinity. Male students were expected to exhibit what Ms. Perry called "gangster-fronting behaviors" in order to be respected (Lei, 2003)—or at the least to not be denigrated as gay. Simultaneously, however, the response to Lao male students who took up urban style as part of their identity was one of puzzlement. Here, discourses of what it means to be male and what it means to be Asian American collided and competed. To be considered "male," young men were expected to take up urban, hip-hop style; but to be viewed as "Asian American," the young men were expected to *not* take up hip-hop aesthetics. For young Asian American men at Dynamic, these were irreconcilable options.

These moments of bewilderment provide us with critical insight into the temporariness of identity and the role of discourses in the process of identification. In the practices of everyday life—in the ambivalent space of identity—my work suggests that Lao students are navigating and restructuring multiple discourses, to open up new possibilities for what it means to be an urban, Lao American student. As I turn to the stories of three Lao American students I call Kett, Vonechai, and Chintana, I specifically underscore the presence of competing and contradictory identities that push up against restrictive—binary—narratives about what it means to be urban, immigrant students.

Temporary Attachments

KETT

At a pause in our conversation, Kett asks, "Do you believe in Jesus?" Do you believe in God? When I tell him that I do, he states, "Without God, you're nothing." Surprised, I ask him, "Are you serious?" He says "Yes" and then asks "Do you go to church?" I tell him that I don't, but have been thinking about finding a church. Kett immediately says, "You should go to my church. It's called the Lao Evangelical Lutheran Church." I ask him if the church was accepting of all people and of diversity. He enthusiastically replies, "Yeah, yeah. We accept everybody." I then ask, "They're not crazy Christians, are they?" Kett responds by saying "No, oh no. You know how there are liberal Christians and conservative Christians?" I say, "Yes. You're a liberal Christian, right?" To my embarrassment Kett tells me that he is actually a conservative Christian and explains that liberal Christians are "hypocrites" who do not practice what they preach. He continues to share with me the location of the church and to give me two phone numbers that I could call for more information. He emphasizes that I should call him by saying "Call me, okay?" a few times and suggests that I should come to church this Sunday (FN 11/15/01, English 10).

In one of my first encounters with Kett, he asked me if I believed in Jesus. When I told him that I did, he replied "Without God, you're nothing." He then proceeded to invite me to attend his church, going so far as to give me its address and phone number. In the course of my research at Dynamic High, I observed Kett telling classmates about the greatness of God and the incredible impact of Christian faith on his life. In our conversations, he continually affirmed the ways in which Christianity changed his perspective on and experiences with life and education. Kett explained his transformation in this way:

> *Kett*: Oh, I used to cuss and joke around and saying bad things. . . . Just be clowning like joking in a bad way. And don't think at all. And don't do nothing for other people like care about them and stuff. I don't, I'm not into that. I really didn't care about family, and now I care about everything, the things that I do and other people too.

Since his sophomore year, Kett has stopped "clowning" at school. Instead, he is so worried and saddened by the lifestyles of his friends that "tears come to [his] eyes" when he thinks about them.

Kett's identity as a Christian is striking because it stands in contrast to the dominance of Buddhism in the identities and lives of ethnic Lao and Lao Americans. According to Krulfeld (1994), the centrality of Buddhism for Lao men is evident by the fact that in Laos the majority of men join the monastery for at least a short period of time in their lives. However, for Kett, since the end of his freshman year, Christianity has played an essential role in his life. The extent of his involvement with his church was impressive. He lived in the home of the pastor of his church and aspired to become a member of the clergy. A few evenings of his week were set aside for practice with the church band, in which he played the drums. The weekends were dedicated to making phone calls and providing transportation to encourage and enable community members to attend Sunday service. Kett described his responsibilities in this way:

Kett: And Sundays, get up in the morning at eight. Get ready. Call people, some of the people and then go in the service. If I don't go in to the adult service before the youth service I just go pick up people and, you know, call them, 'Y'all coming?' Like ask them if they coming. If they coming we go pick them up. But most of the time I'm always in the service. And after the service I call people again, if they coming or not, go pick them up.

When Kett was not giving rides to church on Sundays, he led the youth service and afterward also attended the adult service. When I attended church services, I observed him in leadership roles such as welcoming members of the congregation and leading prayers. According to Kett, this work was a way for him "to serve the Lord and to show [members] how to be the Light, the Light to others—a role model."

In addition to transforming his relationships with his family and friends, Kett's identity as a Christian also affected his education. Kett told me that since the end of his freshman year in high school, he has worked to be a good person and student. As he shared, "I was praying, praying God know I want to take school seriously and I want to serve him more and to keep myself praying at home." A testament to this "serious" attitude toward school included good grades and making the B Honor Roll his sophomore and junior years at Dynamic. He was especially proud of this achievement:

> *Kett is acting very nonchalant toward me today. Unlike other days, he isn't expressive about being glad that I am in his class. However, before class starts, he goes out of the way to walk to the back of the room where I'm sitting to show me the silver card he received for getting on the B Honor Roll.[2] I tell him the accomplishment is wonderful and that I'm proud of him. Kett nods, beams at me, and goes back to his seat. At his desk he sees that the girl sitting in front of him has an Honor Roll t-shirt. He asks her if she's on the Honor Roll. When she confirms this, he proudly takes out his silver card from his back pocket and tells her that he's on the B Honor Roll* (FN 12/10/01, English 11).

For Kett, getting good grades was important because he wanted to be a good role model. He explained to me, "If I don't pass and stuff, and if I show a bad example, you know getting bad grades—How I'm supposed to be a leader to others?"

Kett's identity as a student and person could not be defined simply as a "good student" or "good Christian." One way he illustrated the ambivalence of his identity and blurred discrete notions of good/bad and Christian/non-Christian was in his appearance. His clothes of choice were oversized t-shirts or football jerseys and extremely baggy jeans that he sagged well below his waistline, exposing boxer shorts. Combined with his shaved head, the overall impression that Kett exuded was of a "tough" young man with few academic aspirations. That is, Kett exemplified Lao students whom Ms. Perry described as "gangster-fronting." Consider Ms. Anderson's remarks:

> *Ms. Anderson:* Kett is a great example of a kid who has no clue what his identity is. I mean he sometimes does stuff that's representing for a gang. He'll walk around with a rag hanging out of his pocket, and yet then he'll, I mean in his journals last year he used to write about church *all the time.* Like he's *really,* seemingly really religious or he has this part of his identity that's like really religious. Yet, he obviously has this other pull of potentially getting kind of drawn into gang-related stuff, and kind of trying to be this cool [person]. I don't know. He just strikes me as a kid who's *really* having some serious identity issues and not really knowing what direction he's going to go.

Indeed, as Kett walked around the school "with a rag hanging out of his pocket," while simultaneously preaching the goodness of God, he disrupted dominant understandings of what it meant to be a "good Christian" and "good student." Bewildered by Kett's identity claims, Ms. Anderson saw his struggles as being pulled on one hand by a Christian identity and on the other hand by a gang identity. His identity options are reduced to two paths, where, according to Ms. Anderson, Kett did "not really know what direction he's going to go." From this perspective, it does not make sense that such antagonistic identities can coexist. I suggest that given the range of discourses that are available to us in the process of identification, identities are *necessarily* multiple, contradictory, and unresolved.

Despite assertions that he was no longer "clowning" around and desired to "take school seriously," Kett also admitted that this was difficult. Part of his identity struggles involved trying to be consistent about how he behaved in church and how he behaved in school:

> *Kett:* In church I'm more adult and stuff, everywhere I go. And in school it's just—I'm trying to be mature—and it's

hard. . . . It's just other kids want to draw you into the things they be doing. But I know that *I have to get myself away from that.* And, it's just different 'cause *I could be way, way better here [church] and not that much in school* (my emphasis).

Kett's identity was informed by competing discourses of what it means to be a Christian as well as the attractiveness of "gang-related stuff." In the above comment, Kett alluded to his identity shifting across the contexts of church and school. As he shared, at church he was "more adult and stuff" while at school, it was difficult for him to be mature. To be sure, much like Ms. Anderson, Kett wanted to choose "one path" of a unitary identity. In his struggle with ambiguous, conflicting identities, Kett imagined that he could achieve a cohesive identity by getting away from the bad constitutive influences of the school.

As Kett attempted to behave in ways more consistent with his Christian identity, he came up against competing impulses and messages of "other kids [who] want to draw [him] into the things they be doing." Kett's identity negotiations were not and never can be complete. That is, his negotiations are not as simple and final as choosing one discourse, to go in one direction. As Kett attempted to embrace a Christian identity, traces of his old, "clowning" self remained. In my research, at one moment I witnessed a teacher warning him for having a blue bandana hanging from his back pocket, at another I observed him exhorting the goodness of God to his school peers, and yet at another moment I saw him being sent out of the classroom for misbehaving. On some occasions, I even witnessed Kett poised to simultaneously take up contradictory positions of responsible, church "adult" and truant, school "kid" in the spaces of Dynamic:

> As I walk down the hall toward the stairs, I see Kett in the doorway of the intern teachers' office. When he sees me, he stops talking to the teachers, closes the door, and walks over to where I am standing. I ask him about the class he is scheduled to be in, and he says that he's supposed to be at second lunch. Surprised, I tell Kett that I haven't seen him down there. He replies that he usually doesn't go to lunch because he's "too shy." Instead, Kett shares that he usually goes into Mr. Howard's room, a computer teacher that he had last year or walks around trying to "reach out" to students about God (FN, 12/19/01, Hallway).

Even as Kett played hooky by skipping his assigned lunch hour to roam the halls, he did not unequivocally claim an identity of a "kid" who got into trouble. His identity was fragmented, as he also took up discourses of an "adult" Christian who wanted to "reach out" to share his religious faith with other students.

As we consider the experiences of Kett it is important to note that what happens in identity work is not merely a process of erasure, where something (e.g., one identity as a Christian) overpowers and purges another (e.g., an identity as a goof-off or bad student). Instead, the ambivalence of identity "emphasize[s] the incommensurable elements—the stubborn chunks" that do not go away (Bhabha, 1994, p. 219). In Kett's case, his identity cannot neatly fit into our normative understanding of a "good student" or "Christian" because of the way he dresses and goofs off in school. Simultaneously, his identity as a goof-off or student who may be "drawn into gang-related stuff" does not correspond to notions of a "good student" or "Christian." Kett bore "traces" of the "good student" and "good Christian" as well as traces of "goof-off" and "bad student." Significantly, his identity is not the One or the Other, but "something different, something new and unrecognizable" (Bhabha, 1990, p. 211)

VONECHAI

When I introduced myself to Vonechai and explained that I was doing research at her school, she initiated a handshake greeting by offering me her hand. This gesture of adult formality and sophistication was repeated in her appearance and mannerisms. It foreshadowed a characteristic of Vonechai's identity that was one of the most striking and contentious aspects of her identity work. More so than the majority of the students and adults at the school, Vonechai's hair was coiffed just right and her clothes coordinated completely. As Vonechai explained to me, she is "the queen of preps":

> *Vonechai*: Let's just make this clear, I am the queen of preps supposedly. . . . All my friends, they're like, "You're so preppy. First time I met you, you were just the biggest prep" (laughs). Because like the clothes I wear, I usually shop at The Gap, Nieman Marcus, Bloomingdales, Nordstrom, Express, The Limited, J. Crew, Banana Republic, all the really preppy stores. . . . I am a slacks, blouse, button-down kind of girl, and that's The Gap, and that's The Limited. I'm sometimes kind of fancy, jazzy. I like to look pretty. I'm a girly girl. So Express, that's Express to me and Bloomingdales. And sometimes I just want to look elegant, and that's Bloomingdales, that's Sax Fifth Avenue and stuff like that.

While other students at the school usually wore jeans and t-shirts, Vonechai's outfits typically consisted of nice khakis or slacks and button-down shirts. As she topped these shirts with vests or flipped up the collars of her polo shirts, Vonechai reflected the middle- to upper-middle-class White, Anglo-Saxon Protestant (WASP) images of J. Crew, Polo Ralph Lauren, and Banana Republic models.

Vonechai's material embodiment of upper-middle-class background contrasted starkly with her own family background. Similar to the other Lao American students and many of the students at Dynamic, her family was composed of poor, first-generation immigrants. She lived in a working-class area of the city that was close to, but not in the immediate neighborhood of the school. Her family's home was modestly furnished, the mismatch of furniture strikingly similar to the homes of other Lao students I visited. When I stepped through the front door into Vonechai's home, I had to be careful to avoid stepping on the various dress shoes, tennis shoes, and slippers that were piled on the entryway floor. Facing the doorway was a flight of stairs with carpeted steps covered with clear plastic to thwart the accumulation of dirt and stains. To the right of the entrance was the living room, furnished only with a couch that was pushed up against the wall facing the door. The mantle on the far side of the room immediately drew my attention. In the sparsely decorated home, the mantle stood out because it featured an altar with two black-and-white photographs of a man and a woman, a bowl of fruit, incense sticks, and miscellaneous gold-colored ornaments.

In the fragmented, multilayers of Vonechai's identity, her preppy WASP image coexisted with her Buddhist, low-income, immigrant background. Despite appearances that replicated middle-class, White American society, Vonechai was adamant about her identity as a Lao person:

> *Vonechai*: It means that when I sit down to the table the food I primarily eat is Laotian food. The culture that I follow is Laotian. The family that I am in is Laotian. The beliefs that I have are those of many Laotian people. The religion [Buddhism] is one that is found in the Laotian culture for the most part. So, I may be Americanized, but when I go home and when I look deep inside I'm Laotian. That's who I see myself as. I don't see myself as American, you know. Although I am, I am a citizen of this country, yes, but I mean that doesn't change the fact that yes, of course, I am

American. . . . But just to me, I feel Laotian. I feel like, that's
how I identify myself.

Even as Vonechai drew on the ideas and images of middle-class, White
society in her identity work, she maintained that she was Lao. In the
above excerpt, Vonechai alludes to the incongruity of her identity as
someone who is very "Americanized" in mannerisms and appearances,
but whose perspectives and daily practices are informed by Buddhist
religious beliefs and Lao background. At the same time, there was
indication that Vonechai was struggling to produce a unitary, consistent
storyline (Davies, 2000) as a Lao person. As she attempted to reconcile
the incongruity of her identities, she vacillated between declarations of
"I may be Americanized," "I don't see myself as American," and "that
doesn't change the fact that yes, of course, I am American."

And yet, Vonechai was unlike most of the Lao immigrant (and
other urban) students at the school. She read fashion magazines such
as *Vogue* and *Cosmopolitan*. She owned a cell phone which she took out
frequently at school to check for messages. In our conversations about
clothes, she pointed to actors such as Gwyneth Paltrow, Lucy Liu, Lisa
Ling, and Selma Hayek as role models, stressing that "Gwyneth Paltrow
is my ultimate—love the way she dresses." Indeed, although she considered herself to be Lao, Vonechai recognized that she was different
from the majority of the Lao American students at the school. She
talked at length about clothing to make this point:

> *Vonechai*: I wear a lot of clothes that I don't see a lot of
> Laotian people wearing. . . . I don't see a lot of Laotian
> girls wearing chinos or khakis or just a lot of the clothes
> I wear. I've always seen it as *present* yourself—be who you
> are and show who you are. In a way, I was kind of raised
> conservative, in the sense that you don't show everything
> and you're proper or whatever. I like the clothes. I like the
> way they look. I like the styles. And it's not so weird where
> all my clothes are tattered and you can see my stomach and
> everything is just hanging and stuff like that. I mean I pick
> clothes that I think look, will look good on me. And I pick
> clothes that I like the style of and stuff that's classic.

According to Vonechai, one reason she is different from the other Lao
American girls is due to the fact that she "was kind of raised conservative." As a result, she wears clothes that are "classic" rather than "tattered"
and show her "stomach and [where] everything is just hanging."

Even though Vonechai took up the storyline of a "conservative" upbringing and embodied it with her clothing preferences, she did not take up this narrative in other physical aspects of walking, talking, and behavior. For example, Vonechai's identity as a female student was inconsistent with dominant discourses of Asian American women as quiet and passive (Lee, 1996; Prasso, 2005). While the majority of the Lao American female students at the school hung out primarily with other Lao girls with a few other friends who were Hmong or White, Vonechai's friends included African American, White American, and Hmong American boys and girls. During my time at Dynamic High, I never saw her with a Lao American female student. As we walked through the halls together, I witnessed her greeting and being greeted by students from all racial groups.

In contrast to the reserved—conservative—manner of other Lao American female students such as Lori and Mindy, Vonechai was effusive and loud in speech and actions. Remarking on this difference, she commented:

> *Vonechai*: Well, I think that the difference between me and a lot of the Laotian students in my school is the fact that I get out there. I really (laughs)—I'm one of those people that just would jump in and "Meee, meee, pick me!" There aren't a lot of Asian girls who will do that, just stand up and start dancing in front of their class (laughs). I mean, I get out there and I yell. I try to lead. I try to be active.

Vonechai's strong presence and desire to be active and "try to lead" at Dynamic High manifested daily in the way she confidently moved through the school and related with peers and teachers. Consider a class interaction that I observed:

> *Vonechai overheard a heated discussion that Aaron was having with Jessica at the table behind ours, and asks them about it. When they tell her that they're talking about the Civics teacher's "ridiculous" essay rules, she joins in with passion. Vonechai stands up and loudly states that his method was "stupid" and that it calls for forgetting all that she learned about writing an essay. Jessica and Vonechai are the only students who are standing and talking avidly. Vonechai adds to the commotion by hitting the back of her right hand on the palm of her left hand several times for emphasis. I notice that in contrast to Xay and Nikhong, [two other Lao students] who are sitting quietly at their own table, not talking to*

anyone, Vonechai is vocal and freely expresses her opinions (FN
10/2/01, Pre-IB Geometry).

This passionate, outgoing personality that boldly labeled the pedagogy
of a teacher as "stupid" was especially suitable for school leadership
activities. In middle school, she was president of the student council
at her school as well as the president of the city-wide student organization. Just a 9th-grader in my year at Dynamic High, Vonechai
was already involved in extracurricular activities such as the Student
Council. Indeed, as she explained the strength of her persona, she
proudly shared: "When I walked into Dynamic, they already knew who
I was." According to Vonechai, while "half the kids don't even know
who the principal is," she knew because during a summer activity at
the school, "[h]e came up to [her and said], "Hi, I'm Mr. Gibson. I'm
the principal of Dynamic High."

Similar to the "gangster-fronting behaviors" of Lao American
male students that were inconsistent with dominant discourses of Asian
American men, Vonechai's identity also collided with expectations of
how she should look and act as a Lao American female. She explained
the conflict in this way:

> *Vonechai*: Because I think a lot of them see it as being Lao-
> tian, I have to act a certain way like other Laotian do. But
> not like the Hmong kids or not like the White kids or the
> Black kids, but like Laotians do. And in a way I'm kind of
> chastised for that, because of the fact that, you know, like
> I am claimed *not* to be Laotian, because of the fact that I
> don't act that way.
>
> *BN*: People say you're not Laotian because you don't act a
> certain way?
>
> *Vonechai*: Well, people don't think I am. They're like, "You're
> Laotian?" I'm like "Yeah." And they don't see that. Because
> I don't act a certain way or because I *do* jump, yell, scream
> and really try to be out there. . . . I *like* being the loudest
> in the class.

In these comments, Vonechai alluded to the controlling storylines about
how students should behave as racial and ethnic individuals. There
are specific expectations for performing a "Lao," "Hmong," "White,"
or "Black" identity. According to Vonechai, as a Lao student, she is

required to follow a prescribed pattern of behaviors, "to act a certain way like other Laotian do." She is *not* supposed to jump, scream, and be generally loud. Her failure to conform to the category in which she was positioned resulted in "being kind of chastised."

Additionally, racial and ethnic expectations of identity intersected with gender expectations. As Vonechai clearly articulated in an interview, her identity constructions challenged prevalent discourses of the "Asian girl":

> *Vonechai:* The Asian girl stereotype. I'm supposed to be quiet, which of course you know I am not at all. All I have to say is that one time in Civics: Dance moves. Thank you. *But I'm supposed to be sweet. Sometimes I can be a total bitch* (laughs). And I'm supposed to be quiet and nice and get good grades, when normally I'm the loudest person in the class. My grades are mediocre (my emphasis).

Referring to the Asian American model minority stereotype (see, e.g., Lee, 1996), Vonechai acknowledges that she is "supposed to be quiet and nice and get good grades." Even though she recognized the position to which she was hailed—that she is "supposed to be sweet"—Vonechai instead willfully claimed another storyline. Contrary to expectations, she was loud, flamboyant, opinionated—or as she put it, "a total bitch" at times.

While Lei (2003) found that the "loud Black girls" in her study (cf. Fordham, 1993) were disciplined for not taking up the regulative ideals of White femininity, Vonechai was disciplined—chastised—for not conforming to prescribed images of Asian femininity (i.e., quiet and passive). Because she did not comply with the expected conduct of an Asian woman, her aural and physical visibility was considered to be "Black." Remarking on this, Vonechai shared: "The way I choose to act and walk and talk and speak, that's not Laotian and there's a difference. And today, somebody said something like, 'Why does Vonechai try to act Black?' in 6th hour." At Dynamic High, the discursive practices that classified Vonechai as a particular kind of subject were not simply benign, but were also confining and punitive. As an Asian American female, dominant discourses limited her identity to options of quiet, sweet, and passive. Similar to accusations that Mindy was trying to be "Hmong," Vonechai's failure to comply with dominant storylines resulted in allegations that she was trying to be "Black."

The reading of Vonechai as "Black" is also noteworthy in light of the incongruity of racial markers of her fashion and behavior. In the discursive space of identity, Vonechai drew on contrasting ideas and images that have been ingrained as discretely "White," "Black," and "Asian." Her identity work included inconsistencies of a low-income immigrant, who prefers preppy clothes of stereotypic White, middle-class society, but also takes up dispositions of "loud Black girls." As a social relation (Yon, 2000), her race may be read as ambivalent because she associated with all racial groups at the school. As what Yon (2000) calls a "positivity" or essentialist concept, Vonechai's race is both White and Black, because of her preppy fashion and loud behavior respectively. And yet, as we saw above, Vonechai is insistent that she is Lao. The ambivalence of Vonechai's identity raises the question: Should we consider Vonechai to be Asian, Black, or White? I suggest that she exceeds the three discrete categories, and is all and more.

CHINTANA

I was a little surprised that Chintana agreed to participate in my research. On first impressions, she appeared to be indifferent to everyone and everything. In the hallways of Dynamic, I usually saw her sauntering along without smiling, talking to very few people. In her classes, she moved in and out of social engagement, as students and teachers attempted to connect with her. In all things, Chintana conveyed an air of nonchalance. Almost immediately though, I could tell that other students considered Chintana to be popular. She regularly wore trendy, tight jeans and small, fitted t-shirts. Large, gold hoop earrings and numerous gold-colored bangles usually completed her outfit. Like some of Asian American girls at the school, her long black hair was streaked with caramel blonde highlights. In her demeanor and appearance, Chintana was unlike dominant images of "good" students. As I found out, this incongruity was a theme in other aspects of her experiences and identity.

Since Chintana was a young child, her mother has urged her to avoid friendships with other Lao children. This was because her mother was concerned that she would get involved with Lao gangs like her older sister, three older brothers, and many of the Lao kids in her neighborhood. As Chintana shared with me, the influence of gangs has been a significant part of her life:

> *Chintana:* I grew up around [gangs] but the only people I ever really hung out with was my family that were Lao, like my cousins and stuff. I think part of it is because when my sister and all them, my brothers, were young they got in a lot of trouble. All from Lao kids, how they got into gangs

and stuff. And my mom used to tell me not to hang around so many kids or whatever. They just do different things that I don't. Like, a lot of the Asian girls are like into gangs and stuff. So I don't really care about that.

According to Chintana, she has "seen everything firsthand." Through the activities of her older siblings, she was exposed to gangs for most of her young life. During her childhood, a friend of her brother was shot in the head, and opposing gang members shot at her house on several occasions. The summer before I started my research, one of Chintana's brothers was shot and killed in a gang-related incident. Another brother served time in prison for his gang activities. All of her siblings dropped out of high school due to their involvement in gangs.

Given the presence of gangs in Chintana's life, one could simplistically frame her identity within discourses of urban dysfunction. However, Chintana has heeded her mother's supplications and avoided gang involvement. Since middle school, she has been best friends with a high-achieving, mixed-race Korean American–African American student. At Dynamic High, while Chintana was enrolled in the Open Program, her best friend was in the International Baccalaureate Program. During my research, the spring of their junior year, both Chintana and her best friend were inducted into the National Honor Society (NHS). In our conversations, she echoed the discourse of achievement and shared that she wanted to be the first person in her family to attend college. Chintana's success was especially notable to Mr. Sullivan, her English teacher:

> *Mr. Sullivan*: Bright young lady, very capable. If she keeps her head, she can go as far as she wants to go. And yet, at the same time, Chintana has grown up in pretty abject and severe poverty. Her family is such that her brother is in jail, he might be out now, I'm not sure. The family is sort of split up and fractured. And I think Chintana is trying to figure out, do you stay with what you grew up with, which is this model of man that isn't very positive? Or do you try to go out and find, create something new, which you really don't have any model to work from? You're creating it as you go.

Similar to Ms. Anderson's remarks about Lao American students at Dynamic, Mr. Sullivan believed that Chintana was trying to figure out what kind of person she wanted to be. In the above excerpt, Mr.

Sullivan implied that Chintana has two choices or paths in her decision making. One path would lead her to academic success—to "go as far as she wants to go" by going out to "create something new, which [she doesn't] have any model to work from," and embrace the discourse of the promise of education. The other path would lead her to delinquency—to "stay with what [she] grew up with, which is this model of man that isn't very positive."

Importantly, Mr. Sullivan's observations recognized the changing nature of identity and Chintana's role in identity creation and re-creation. Nonetheless, his observations ultimately reflected and played into the simplification of binary discourses (e.g., good student/bad student, success/failure). I argue that Chintana's ambivalent identity "contests the terms and territories of both" (Bhabha, 1994, p. 28) paths—academically successful student or delinquent—suggested by Mr. Sullivan. Chintana's identity as an urban student was not as straightforward as choosing between gang *or* school achievement discourses. Her identity was not a cohesive identity of a "good student" who has been successful at avoiding gang involvement.

For almost two years, Chintana dated an African American student who was involved in a gang. Her boyfriend was kicked out of school at the end of their freshman year after multiple suspensions and absences. He was considered by teachers to be among the toughest young men they have known. This relationship is important for understanding the ambivalent character of identity for at least two reasons. First, Chintana's romantic involvement with a young man who rejected and was rejected by school was incongruent with her identity as a "good student" and as someone who has worked to avoid gang involvement. Second, our dominant understanding of tough young men involved in gangs positions them as anti-school. However, according Chintana, besides her mother, her boyfriend encouraged her most in her studies. He told her that, "he can see [her] doing something, making something of [herself]."

What makes Chintana's identity as a student even more incomplete is that she did not embrace the discourse of school achievement unequivocally. Consider a conversation we had about college:

Close to the end of the hour, Chee, Chintana, and I are sitting together at a table in front of the classroom. During our conversation, they tell me that they've just registered for classes for next year. Chintana shared that she is taking physics and a pre-calculus math class because Mr. Sullivan told her she needs the two classes if she plans to go to college. She tells me that she doesn't want to take the classes but has to. I ask her if she wants to go to college and she says yes. I then ask, "Then you'll be the first person in your family to go to college?" She casually nods her head and then says, "Yeah, that's why I want to go. But I also don't want to go." When I ask her why she doesn't want to go, she candidly shares, "I'm tired of school. I don't want to go anymore." I try to encourage Chintana, and tell her and Chee that college is very different from high school and that they'll be able to focus on their interests. Chintana replies dejectedly that she doesn't know what she's interested in or what she's good at. Speaking to both girls, I tell them they'll have the chance to figure that out in college as well. I go on to share that what I thought I would end up doing in high school and in college is completely different from what I'm doing now (FN, 2/28/02, Chemistry).

As we talked about college, Chintana shifted—in the same speaking—from a college-going student to a non-college-going student. In one sentence she asserted, "I want to go" so that she can be the first person in her family to go to college. And yet, she immediately also claimed, "But I also don't want to go" because she was tired of school and was unsure about her skills and interests.

Another conversation that I had with Chintana during the time of the National Honor Society induction ceremony is also illustrative of the incompleteness of her anti-school identity. During chemistry class one day, we were casually talking about the NHS ceremony. In her usual way, Chintana spoke with little inflection, seemingly unengaged with the conversation. As we talked Chintana mentioned to me that parents are supposed to attend the ceremony with the inductees. She shared that her mom had to work that night and that she did not have anyone to go to the ceremony with her. I told her I was sorry and asked if students were required to take part in the ceremony. Chintana replied that they were not and then stopped and looked at me. At first, I was unsure of what she wanted me to say. After a brief pause, I hesitantly offered that if she needed an adult to escort her, I would be happy to do so. Immediately, Chintana's face lit up and she told me that she would really like it if I attended the ceremony with her. In the end, Chintana's mother was able to take time off of work and we were able to witness her induction into the Honor Society together. Thus, in some ways, Chintana embraces the discourse of school achievement.

Yet in other ways, Chintana resisted the discourse of school achievement and made fun of students who were "nerds" and conformed to messages of school engagement. For instance, during one part of our interview she told me that she did not want to be a "nerd." As she derisively called another Lao student a "nerd," Chintana explained her rationale for the label: "Cause she does like other extracurricular activities outside of school too I know. I know she's in some ad for drugs or something. She does all that crap." And yet, these assertions that school involvement was "crap" and that she did not want to be a "nerd" were not final declarations of identity. A few minutes later in the interview, Chintana contradictorily boasted that her best friend was a nerd: "Cause she overachieves. She knows it. She calls herself a nerd. I call her a nerd all the time. That's good though. We're all proud of her, 'cause she's going to be somebody." In the ambivalence of identity, Chintana moved from rejecting school achievement as "crap" in one moment to embracing it as a way to become "somebody" in another moment.

Indeed, after she asserted that extracurricular activities were "crap," I reminded her that she was involved in the National Honor Society. In response, Chintana laughed and explained that she joined the NHS because she wanted the "extra things on [her] robe" when she graduated "so [she] can put it on [her] application for college" and "just so everybody knows [she] was smart." Chintana not only wanted to be able to list membership in the National Honor Society in her college application, but moreover, her participation in the ceremonial components of the honor was also important. As Chintana drew on disparate storylines in her identity work, she destabilized the relationship between "Me" and "Not Me." She was not simply "pro-school" *or* "anti-school" but both and more. Her claims to oppositional positions of "nerd" and "not nerd" blurred normative, finite categories of identity.

In the ambivalent space of identity, Chintana's identity choices are not merely those between dual identities of someone who embraces or resists school, or someone who embraces or resists gangs. As Davies (1993) cogently explains,

> [w]ho we take ourselves to be at any one point in time depends on the available storylines we have to make sense out of . . . being-in-the-world, along with the legitimacy and status accorded to those storylines by others (p. 4).

The storylines of Chintana's identity shifted continuously as she moved between available, conflicting discourses. Her identity as an urban, immigrant student was fractured and incomplete, neither fully "good" nor fully "bad." The partitioning of Chintana's identity is not binary, but multiple and subdivided (Maira, 2002). For example, within the multilayers of an academic identity, Chintana's identity claims included that as an Honor Student, a student who was emphatically not a nerd, and someone who also wanted to be viewed as a smart student. Moreover, Chintana's position toward school achievement—as she vacillated between reflecting and resisting the achievement discourse—is illustrative of the incongruous elements of urban student identities that are informed by a variety of discourses. Her ambivalent identity tells us that one may resist involvement in gang activity, achieve good grades in school—but contradictorily still disavow school success, have siblings involved in gangs, and be in a relationship with a gang member. Thus, as multiple discourses "attempt to 'interpellate,' speak to us, or hail us" (Hall, 1996, p. 5) we speak back with *multiple* responses.

In this chapter we saw that urban, immigrant students such as Chintana, Vonechai, and Kett are drawing on a range of disparate, conflictual discourses in their identity work. For Lao American students at Dynamic High, various available discourses provided them "with multiple layers of contradictory meanings that are inscribed in their bodies and in their conscious and unconscious minds" about who they are or can be (Davies, 1993, p. 13). Instead of the finality of identity categories such as "bad student," "nerd," or "preppy," Lao student identities are conflictual and unresolved. As we saw, in the ambivalence of identity, students moved through a range of positionings—even in the same conversation (Davies, 2000). Importantly, the "multiple layers of contradictory meanings" in the identities of Kett, Chintana, and Vonechai demonstrate that the finality set forth by discrete, binary categories of identity will always be premature.

6

Resisting Resolution

> I see this moving about as a strategy that affirms "you know me/I know you" while pointing insistently to the interested partialness of these knowings; and constantly reminding us that "you can't know me/I can't know you" while unsettling every definition of knowing arrived at.
>
> —Elizabeth Ellsworth, "Why doesn't this feel empowering?"

One of the questions that I continually asked during the data collection, analysis, and writing of my research included: How are the experiences of Lao American students different from those of other urban students? In relation, it could also be asked: How are the experiences of Lao students different from other immigrant students? Put another way, I wondered how the ethnic identity of my participants made their experiences uniquely different from other urban and immigrant students. I have come to understand that what was paramount in the identity struggles of my Lao participants were the multiplicity, variability, and inconsistency of their identities. This ambivalence of identity resists conceptualizations of discrete, binary discourses that put the ethnic identity of the students at one end of the spectrum and another identity at the other end. My study suggests that, while research explicating differences between immigrants and dominant U.S. society has been important, the bicultural framework does not pay enough attention to the ways that the experiences of students as immigrants in U.S. schools and society *intersect* with their experiences as adolescents, urban students, and racial and ethnic minorities, among other identities.

When immigrant students quarrel with parents about dyeing their hair, wearing skirts that are too short, or listening to music that is too loud, these conflicts are simultaneously about being a teenager and being an immigrant. Likewise, when immigrant students struggle with the lure of gangs, how to afford trendy clothes they want, or getting enough meals each day, these issues are at once about being disenfranchised, an urban youth, and an immigrant. Understanding these tensions only as binary struggles between an immigrant culture and U.S. culture undermines the fluidity of experiences that I believe the "between two worlds" research has attempted to articulate. It is worth reiterating that framing immigrant experiences only as conflicts between the first-generation and second-generation emphasizes familial culpability in the challenges faced by immigrants and minimizes the responsibility of the cultural politics of difference (Lowe, 1996). It overlooks the ways discourses about gender, race, ethnicity, sexuality, class, and other dimensions of difference impact what it means to be an immigrant in U.S. schools and society. As we saw, Lao American students at Dynamic High were racialized as "Asian" and simultaneously misrecognized as "Chinese" and "Hmong." For Lao male students in particular, their identities were simultaneously influenced by racialized discourses of what it means to be Asian American (i.e., not gangster) and gendered discourses of what it means to be male at the school (i.e., stylized in hip-hop clothes).

Descriptors such as "immigrant," "adolescent," "urban," or "Asian" mask contradictions *within* the individual categories as well as the complex relationship *between* categories that inhere in the everyday realities of identity work. The temporariness of Vonechai's attachments as a low-income student who identified as Lao and Buddhist, but embraced discourses of middle-class, White, Protestant preppiness at the same time that she took up what peers called "Black" mannerisms exceeds categories of "Lao," White," or "Black." Chintana's vacillation between reflecting the message of academic diligence and belittling school engagement as "crap" points to the instability of discrete categories such as "good student" or "bad student." Chintana is both and more. Similarly, as a Lao immigrant who is a devout Christian, but has "gangster-fronting" behaviors and yet is on the Honor Roll, Kett reveals the inadequacy of definitive categories such as "Christian," "gangster," or "honor student."

The propensity toward classification repeats the inscription of restrictive ideas about who we are or should be as individuals. In Chapter 2, we saw urban schools and communities reduced to dysfunctional notions of the "jungle" or "zoo" that are controlled by violence and chaos. Questions such as "Do you have metal detectors?" as well as "rags to riches" transformational stories in different ways redeployed old storylines of urban schools as spaces of disorder and failure. In Chapter 3, we examined the categorization of urban student identities at one extreme as "war babies" who needed the school for "shelter" from supposedly unstable lives and neighborhoods; and at the other extreme as resilient individuals able to "beat the odds" despite adverse circumstances. Similarly, in Chapter 4 we saw the identities of Lao American students essentialized and misrecognized as "Chinese" and "Hmong," and constrained by the power of longstanding discourses about what it means to be an individual of Asian heritage.

The discursive practices through which identities are constituted are not just "out there" circulating harmlessly. They are taken up by us and others within social practices and relations, and as such, are potentially dangerous (Britzman, 1998; Davies, 2000; Taylor, 1994). According to Taylor (1994), within social relations our identities are prospective sites of oppression and even captivity. As the experiences of Lori and Mindy illustrated, the everyday practices and interactions with school peers, teachers, and parents opened up opportunities not only for identification, but also for tensions and oppression. The incoherence and incongruities of identity open up a space not only for newness to come into the world (Bhabha, 1994), but also opportunities for disagreements that alienate, denigrate, and confine who students are and want to become. Part of this dilemma comes from the physical, emotional, and psychic commitments that we make by claiming certain storylines for our subject positions. Indeed, as we saw, students like Vonechai and Kett made physical investments in embodying discourses through the ways they dressed, walked, talked, and interacted with others. There are no guarantees, however, that our identity investments will be supported by peers, parents, and others. In the double movement of identity, our images of and desires for ourselves may collide with the external, coercive narratives of others. For Lao American students like Vonechai, Lori, and Mindy, the (mis)taking—rejection—of their identities was not only at a theoretical level, but also in the material realities of disciplinary acts of marginalization.

And yet, it is not only teachers, staff, peers, and parents who are misreading or are confused about the identities of Lao American students. The Lao students themselves are uncertain about who they are or want to be. They draw on a whole range of (competing) discourses to make sense of their identities. As illustrated by Vonechai's "conservative" clothing preferences and boisterous personality, identity claims are conflictual, made in multiple directions. As demonstrated by the experiences of Chintana and Kett as urban students who neither entirely embraced nor entirely rejected the gang or school achievement discourses, identities are neither consistent nor finite. In the ambivalence of identity, the boundaries between "Me" and "Not Me" are continually blurred and put into question. Bhabha (1994) explains the difficulty of articulating a "real" identity in this way: "the discursive space from which *The real Me* emerges (initially as an assertion of the authenticity of the person) and then lingers on to be reverberated—*The real Me?*—as a questioning of identity" (p. 49). In other words, as a discursive declaration of a unitary true self, the "Real Me" appears in the beginning as a statement of fact. But in the space where it echoes back, the statement becomes a question for the speaker. The attempt to assert the authenticity of identity ultimately reveals the uncertainty and incompleteness of the articulation.

We reach and aspire, though, toward the simplicity and ease of unitary, consistent stories—for ourselves as well as for others. At Dynamic, this occurred in discursive practices that negated the multiplicity of what it means to be an Asian immigrant. The fractures of identity were distilled into one-dimensional ideas of "celebrating" cultures and labels that homogenized all Asian ethnic groups as "Chinese" or "Hmong." We also heard the resistance to contradictions and uncertainty in the bewilderment of teachers such as Mr. Sullivan and Ms. Anderson, who wanted students like Chintana and Kett to choose one direction, rather than vacillate between unresolved, competing identities. In Vonechai's case, she was chastised for claiming an incoherent identity of a Lao student "trying to be Black." Students like Kett also struggled with the inconsistencies of identity and longed for the coherence of a mature, "adult" Christian identity. He imagined that he "could be way, way better" if he were only at church, away from the influence of the "kids" at school.

Remarking on the problems of tidy, coherent stories of urban identities and experiences, Michelle Fine and Lois Weis (1998) suggest that "we need to invent an intellectual stance in which structural oppression, passion, social movements, evidence of strength, health, and 'damage' can all be recognized without erasing essential features of the complex story that constitutes urban life and poverty" (p. 286). At Dynamic High, we saw the inadequacy of unitary, simplistic stories that framed the identities and experiences of urban, immigrant students within binary categories of good/bad, traditional/modern, and successful/unsuccessful. And yet, is it possible to think in ways that do not rely on binary frameworks? Given the nature of language, do we not *always* and *already* think, function, and make meaning through binaries? If this is the case, one way forward is to continuously question or trouble binary categories even as we work within them. In other words, we need to constantly underscore the *temporariness* of identity.

Specifically, my work suggests that considering the identities of immigrant students through the conceptual lens of *ambivalence* is a way toward an "intellectual stance" that is able to unsettle the tidiness of binaries. Ambivalence allows us to emphasize the ways that identity is conflictual, partial and unresolved. It accounts for the complexities that are produced when immigrant students, their teachers and peers, and others draw on a multiplicity of discourses in the process of identification. From this perspective, instead of a place for resolution, identity is a site "for multiplying and making more complex the subject positions possible, visible and legitimate" (Ellsworth, 1989, p. 321).

Uncertainty of Teachers

So far, I have focused on illuminating the various discourses and practices that informed and shaped the identities of urban, Lao American students at Dynamic High School. In doing so, I highlighted the discursive practices of teachers and staff that confined the identities of students into simplistic categories that reinscribed narratives of urban pathology as well as feel-good stories of urban triumph. Following Britzman (2000), I want "to hold tightly to the ethic of not producing [the participants in my study] as persons to blame or as heroes of resistance" (p. 32). Just as I have argued for the messiness of conflictual urban, immigrant student identities, I want to also recognize the precarious location of teacher identities. In the ambivalent space of identity, students are not the only ones who occupy contradictory positions. As teachers drew on disparate discourses to make sense of their school, students, and experiences, they also created inconsistent, uncertain identities that complicate—indeed defy—binary frameworks of "good" or "bad" teacher identities.

As we saw, teachers and staff drew on discourses of urban dysfunction as they pointed to unstable, impoverished, "broken" homes to elucidate the experiences of their students. Simultaneously, they summoned discourses of resilience and offered examples of multiple jobs, excellent grades, and other examples of perseverance to tell a "beat the odds" story of success. By and large, these discourses denigrated or romanticized the experiences of urban students and families. Some of the narratives about the lives of students were especially discomforting—if not altogether offensive. The comment by Ms. Perry that I shared in Chapter 5 is illustrative:

> *Ms. Perry:* How can I put this? I sometimes sit and observe other classes, and I've watched Laotian males interact with Black males and it's been interesting. Because I don't know if this is racially based or anything, but I mean maybe it's adolescent male, urban adolescent male (laughs). But I see

the Laotian male trying to act kind of the gangster-fronting behaviors. And some of the Black males kind of seeing them bewildered by this. And kind of checking each other out, *kind of like two dogs of different breeds kind of sniffing and checking each other out.* But kind of trying to act the same. . . . It's all an attempt to fit in (my emphasis).

Surely, Ms. Perry's description of the interactions of African American and Lao American students as "kind of like two dogs of different breeds kind of sniffing and checking each other out" is deeply problematic. The use of "dogs" as a metaphor for students (of color) warrants the categorization of Ms. Perry as a "bad teacher" at best, and even suggests labels of "bigot" or "racist."

Nonetheless, as I argued with students, it is critical to unsettle one-dimensional, unitary discourses that constitute teachers within dualisms of "good" or "bad." Similar to the urban, immigrant students, the identities of teachers are also contradictory and unstable. I knew Ms. Perry to be deeply committed to addressing issues of inequality such as racism, sexism, and homophobia. During the spring she worked with her English classes on a "tolerance" unit over the course of the semester, the first time that she addressed issues of racism, sexism, and homophobia within a whole unit. For the unit on homophobia, for example, reading assignments included a hate crime article, an article from PFLAG (Parents, Families and Friends of Lesbians and Gays), as well as two articles from former Dynamic High students explicating the homophobia they experienced at the school. As she offered an assessment of the unit, Ms. Perry shared responses from students that pushed her to think more complexly about discrimination:

Ms. Perry: The homophobia thing, it was interesting. . . . I had one paper that flat out said, "Gays are wrong. Gays deserve to die." It was written by a White male who is also fiercely against racism. And when I wrote back on his paper, "How can you not discriminate based on race but you're okay with discriminating on sexual orientation?" And he said, "Well it's just morally wrong. People have a choice and in race you don't." So he viewed the sexual orientation as a choice. And I didn't really present a thorough amount of information on homosexuality. So the degree to which they had information about origins of homosexuality and lifestyles and so on, they only had a limited amount. And

that's something I regret, and if I had more time this year
I would have done more.

This statement illustrates and reiterates the discontinuities of identity
on a couple of levels. At one level, it reveals and confirms the incoherence of identity, where a White male student can be anti-racist and
yet homophobic. While the student was "fiercely against racism," he
also believed homosexuality was "just morally wrong." At another level,
it illustrates the complexity of Ms. Perry's identity. As a teacher who
engaged in pedagogical practices that addressed racism, sexism, and
homophobia, she muddles and contradicts the category of a "bigot"
who frames students as "dogs."

   The extent of Ms. Perry's commitment to anti-oppressive education
(Kumashiro, 2002) can be heard in the anxiety and regret in the above
remarks about the amount of time and curriculum materials allotted to
the homophobia unit. In fact, in our conversation she talked at length
about plans to improve the unit the following year by incorporating
the lessons over the course of both academic semesters. Rather than
spend only a few weeks on the unit, integrating it throughout the year
would allow the class "more time to get to know each other." Further,
as Ms. Perry insightfully noted, it would also provide time for her to
"do that synthesis piece" where she could ask about the incongruities:
" 'How can you *not* be racist and then turn around and be homophobic?'
Or, 'How can you be sexist and not be racist?' You know, doing the
contradiction probing." Indeed, just as Ms. Perry's student was situated
in contradictory positions, teachers such as Ms. Perry also come from
multiple, contradictory locations.

   Another facet of the ambivalence of the identities of teachers
included their uncertain understandings of student identities. While
teachers such as Ms. Sanders discursively positioned their students
within discrete, simplistic categories, there was also evidence that she
was unsure of the way she framed her students. Consider her charac-
terization of an African American student as a "man-child":

> *Ms. Sanders:* They're not the kind of challenges that if we
> all had our way and we could structure a good learning
> environment and a good set of experiences for kids, *not the*
> *kinds of things that they should naturally be facing at that age.*
> I have James who's in my second hour class. *He's got a kid*
> *and I mean he's a father. Yeah, he's a sweet, sweet kid. He's kind*
> *of like a man, like a man-child.* He's had to grow up on some

levels 'cause *there's all these sets of areas where he's like a man and then there's all these sets of places where he's just still a kid* (my emphasis).

Recall that Ms. Sanders used the metaphor of "war babies" to describe Dynamic High students in Chapter 3. Her ideas about what it means to be a young person and an adult give preference to a particular understanding of distinctive, age-specific experiences for children and adults. For Ms. Sanders, "a good set of experiences for kids" did not include death, poverty, homelessness, and the other challenges that she saw her students facing. This binary understanding of experiences requires a separation between "adult" and "kid" experiences. What it means to be a "high school student" should not include being a parent or being exposed to death and other hardships. And yet, there were murmurs of uncertainty in her positioning of James. Her description of this sophomore student, who used to be involved in gang activities, vacillates between the storyline of "a father" and a storyline of "a kid" who is "a sweet, sweet kid." While she pointed to elements of his identity that forced James "to grow up on some levels," her positioning wavers. Ms. Sanders acknowledges the ambivalence of a "man-child" identity, where James is "like a man" but then has "all these sets of places where he's just still a kid."

To be sure, I am also guilty of this kind of categorization. There were numerous times during my research when I shared the anxieties of teachers over the "adult" experiences of students. On one occasion, for example, I was having breakfast with Bao and Kia, two Hmong girls who were friends with a couple of my Lao participants. We were talking about my desire to elucidate the experiences of the students at Dynamic when Bao interrupted Kia and pointed to a table 10 feet from us where 6 Hmong girls were sitting. Bao said to me, "You should interview them." When I asked her why, she explained that all of the girls at the table were married and had at least one child. To me, the girls exemplified images of the "average" high school student, with especially stylish hair, makeup, and clothes. I was jarred by the incongruity of the way they looked as young people and the knowledge that they had enormous responsibilities as parents. My assumption that the Hmong girls were single and childless are based on White, middle-class—dominant—storylines of the behaviors and responsibilities of the "average," young, female high school student. I have come to recognize that this dominant script about who adolescent females are and should be confines the identities of urban, immigrant students. Attempts to position students who become pregnant and have children out-of-wedlock within unitary categories invariably depend on inadequate, denigrating binaries of adult/child, normal/not normal, and good girl/bad girl (Luttrell, 2003; Schultz, 2001).

I suggest that, to a certain degree, Dynamic teachers and staff also recognized that urban students like James occupy ambivalent positions as a "man-child." Their attempts to situate students within discrete categories of what it means to be a "student," "child," "parent," or "adult" were accompanied by the anxieties of naming (Bhabha, 1994), where statements of who students are underscored the inadequacy of the unitary categories. What we saw in the discursive practices of teachers and staff is our overriding tendency toward classification—particularly toward dominant, binary discourses—to make sense of urban identities and experiences. Our stories have the propensity to carry an emphatic finality to identities that are much more unresolved and ambivalent. Like the students at Dynamic High, the incongruities of teacher and staff identities cannot be neatly confined within unitary, dualisms of good/bad or racist/anti-racist (cf. Yon, 2000).

Troubling the "Real Me" of Multicultural Education

Similar to many schools in the United States, Dynamic High School symbolically and materially encouraged the celebration and respect for social and cultural differences. This manifested as posters, wall displays, and curricular practices such as special student groups (e.g., Asian Cultural Club) and celebrations of a "month" or a "day" dedicated to different groups (e.g., Asian American History in May, Black History in February, Coming Out Day in October). This contributions approach to multicultural education seeks to "affirm" the experiences of groups by ubiquitously focusing on holidays, heroes, traditions, food, music, and dance as discrete elements of culture and identity. The difference of identity is paraded out and highlighted through isolated "tolerance units," "multicultural weeks," or "history months." This claim to honor and "celebrate diversity" positions and reinforces cultural identity as "exotic," something to be viewed as perhaps curious and quaint, but still "Other" (Burbules, 1997). The exoticization of people, food, aesthetics, and customs, among other things, continues to sustain power hierarchies and constitutive boundaries between "Us" and "Them" (Britzman, 1998; Burbules, 1997; West, 2002).

As an exemplar of this pervasive practice of multicultural education, the Asian Cultural Club embodied an understanding of "cultural identity" defined "in terms of one, shared culture, a sort of a collective 'one true self'" (Hall, 1990, p. 223). But as we saw in Chapter 4, the discontinuities and ruptures of identity refute notions of a "one experience, one identity" of a cultural group (Hall, 1990, p. 225). At Dynamic High, the tensions of identity that Lao students experienced with Hmong students, other Lao students, and their own parents cannot be mollified in practices seeking to "know" or "celebrate" cultures. Multicultural practices of the Asian Show contradictorily reinforced the Othering of Asian American students in general and Lao students in particular. As Britzman (1998) argues, "the lived effects of 'inclusion' are a more obdurate version of sameness and a more polite version of otherness" (p. 87). Indeed, at Dynamic High, the preoccupation with "recognizing" the histories, cultures, and contributions of groups in actuality misrecognized the identities of Lao American students.

Thomas West (2002) reminds us that because "much [of] multicultural discourse continues to represent difference *as diversity*, it often advances pedagogies and curricular reform that elide histories of difference *as alterity*, as the politics of "othering" people for particular reasons" (p. 28, emphasis in original). Diverse customs and diverse lifestyles are not the problem, but the meanings, values, and classifications that are ascribed to the cultural differences (Bhabha, 1999; West, 2002). Cultures and identities thus become categorized as good/bad, modern/traditional, normal/not normal, and us/them. Conceptualizing difference as alterity highlights the way that identity "is constructed across the bar of difference" (Bhabha, 1990, p. 210) and within social relations. As a product of the process of "Othering," cultural difference inscribes meaning into identities for the purpose of inclusion and exclusion (West, 2002). In other words, thinking about the difference of cultures and cultural identities as alterity brings attention to the social (and political) need to make sense of and constitute identities within categories of "Me" and "Not Me."

As we saw at Dynamic High School, the attempt to assuage the marginalization of the cultural differences of the "Other" through multicultural education was an insufficient response to the conflict of difference. However, it is not just that the (well-intentioned) focus on affirmation of multicultural practices contradictorily maintains the difference between "Me" and "Not Me." But, moreover, multicultural education perpetuates the fiction of an essential "Real Me" of minoritized cultures that is separate and distinctive from the hegemonic norm. The trouble with multicultural education is arguably a problem of binary oppositions, where discrete categories of same and different, oppressor and oppressed, or us and them are obstinately renewed (Britzman, 1998). How might theorizing about identity as ambivalent respond to a multicultural education that re-inscribes delegitimizing discourses?

One response to this question is to trouble the myth of the "Real Me" of multiculturalism and cultural identity. In schools and classrooms, this would mean fostering teaching practices that resist resolutions of identity, that make paramount the incoherence and unknowability of identity, and aim to "unsettle readers into a sort of stammering knowing" (Lather, 1997, p. 288) about their and our experiences.

For pedagogy to embrace the ambivalence of identity, we need to engender a multiplicity of options for identifications—along with the uncertainty and unruliness that they bring. Elaborating on the productive possibilities of "reading practices" of identity for a destabilizing "queer pedagogy," Britzman (1998) asks:

> What if one thought about reading practices as problems of opening identifications, of working the capacity to imagine oneself differently precisely in one's encounters with another and in one's encounters with the self? What if how one reads the world turned upon the interest in thinking against one's thoughts, in creating a queer space where old certainties made no sense (p. 85)?

These questions point to ways forward for troubling the "Real Me" of multicultural education (and pedagogies in general). Taking them seriously would require us to stretch toward ways to teach and learn that cultivate myriad choices for identifications, questions our own beliefs, and upends the finality of longstanding, privileged storylines. Fundamental to this pedagogy is the acknowledgment that the boundaries between "Me" and "Not Me" are inventions of our social relations and discursive practices (Davies, 2000; Ellsworth, 2006). Instead of fixed or stable, the distinctions between "Me" and "Not Me" shift, collide, and rupture. Put another way, we need to work toward creating enunciative possibilities for subjectification that move beyond fixed, cohesive choices for our identity work.

In everyday life, working toward the "proliferation of identificatory possibilities" (Britzman, 1998, p. 85) can manifest in a variety of ways. At its simplest, unsettling dualistic categories means paying attention to how we position students. Do we label and finalize urban, immigrant students such as Kett as coherently "gangster-fronting"? Do we classify Vonechai as definitively "Lao"? Likewise, do we categorize students like Chintana as simply "high-achieving"? In the spaces of schools and classrooms, moving beyond simplistic, unitary possibilities could mean actively looking for the contradictions of identity work. What would it mean if we read the identity work of students as temporary attachments?

What would it mean if we read the storylines we tell about ourselves and others as partial narratives? At the least, it might help us to avoid complacency about students we perceive to be "good" or pass judgment (and give up) on those who are "bad."

As we saw in this book, our current dominant discourses about urban schools and students privilege the beliefs, values, and narratives that frequently obscure the complexity of their experiences. In order to be taken up in identification, the discourses, metaphors, and images we draw on to make sense of the world need to be in circulation and available to us (Davies, 2000; Weedon, 1987). Since discourses play an integral role in our identity work, we might open ourselves and students to more complex—as of yet marginalized, unthinkable, unthought—storylines for our identity work. For example, consider the influence of hip-hop in the identity work of Lao American students at Dynamic High. Dominant storylines currently associate and frame hip-hop identities as exclusively misogynistic, violent, and "gangster-fronting" (Abrams, 2007; Ross, 2007). Instead of recirculating these discourses, we might introduce ourselves and students to discourses about hip-hop that include notions of political activism, social criticism, and artistic, poetic expression (Chang, 2005; Watkins, 2006). Such pedagogy acknowledges that culture and identity are continuously constituted and reconstituted in everyday practices, interests, and social relations of urban, immigrant youth and families. It requires engaging ourselves and students in the critical examination of dominant discourses and integrating the interests and lives of students into classroom curriculum and instruction (Ladson-Billings, 1995; Moll & Gonzalez, 2003). Class lessons that delve into the outside school interests of immigrant students and families might reveal, for example, that immigrant adolescents are identifying as hip-hop spoken-word artists. They might further reveal that supposedly "traditional" immigrant communities are having "coming out" parties for gay, lesbian, bisexual, and transgender (GLBT) immigrant youth and adults (Mouacheupao, 2006).

Generating new sites for identification also necessitates unraveling familiar narratives about what it means to be urban, immigrant students. Part of this work involves exposing the *politics* of identity. For minoritized populations such as urban immigrants, cultural identities are imbued with the politics of identity formed at the intersections of race, ethnicity, gender, class, language, and religion, among others. Highlighting the politics involved in cultural difference, Bhabha (1999) argues that difference is not a problem in and of itself. Rather, it only becomes so

because there is some particular issue about the redistribution
of goods between cultures, or the funding of cultures, or the
emergence of minorities in a situation of resources—where
resource or allocation has to go—or the construction of
schools and the decision about whether the school should
be bilingual, trilingual or whatever (p. 16).

Within the spaces of classrooms, exposing the politics of identity may
mean considering the struggle over interests and resources that frame
and racialize urban spaces as Black, primitive, and dangerous (Haymes,
1995). Similarly, we might interrogate stereotypes of immigrants to reveal
the contexts and motivations that undergird narratives about immigrants
as burdens on the U.S. economy. This examination of our current
discursive practices is critical for working past familiar, normative ways
of understanding identity; and essential for elucidating the individual
person as part of an ongoing discursive process (Davies, 2000).

Writing about the efforts of African Americans to combat racializing representations, bell hooks (1992) asserts that the

fundamental task of black critical thinkers has been the
struggle to break with the hegemonic modes of seeing,
thinking, and being that block our capacity to see ourselves
oppositionally, to imagine, describe, and invent ourselves in
ways that are liberatory (p. 2).

This "fundamental task" of African American scholars to break away
from confining, normative "modes of seeing" is also our task as educators. The difficulty of delegitimizing storylines is their availability not
only to others, but also to us, for our identifications. When we speak
as subjects, we also take up as our own the very destructive narratives
that constitute us (Davies, 2000). As this book illustrates, the narratives
that are widely available to urban, immigrant students are confining,
demeaning, and inadequate. What would it mean for educators to
focus on student narratives—competing, alternative narratives? As a
response to dominant discourses, new storylines or counterstories put
forward by students make possible different avenues to reply to oppressive hegemonic discourses of who they are or should be. They allow
students to imagine and construct self-definitions and social identities
that rupture the identities imposed on them by our current dominant
narratives.

Resisting Resolution

For the second consecutive day, Ms. Richardson's chemistry class is in the computer lab in the Media Center. The students are using the Internet to do research for their science project presentations. Ananh and Chintana are sitting on opposite sides of the C-shaped computer alcove, working on projects about Albert Einstein and Avogadro, respectively. Since I can't sit with both Chintana and Ananh, I decide to focus on Ananh today. In place of his usual button-down shirts, Ananh is wearing a dark blue, crew-neck sweater along with Old Navy brand carpenter jeans and black dress shoes. I'm sitting at a row of computers with Ananh to my left and Zer, Kia, and Poua to my right. I talk a little with Zer and Kia, who are working on a project about perfumes, but give most of my attention to Ananh. Just as the students are settling into their work, Ms. Richardson comes over to Ananh and tells him that Chintana won't be able to help him with recycling this afternoon and that he will have to do it alone. He says, "Okay" and then turns to me and asks, "Do you want to help me?" I tell Ananh "Yes" and ask when and where we should meet. Ananh replies that he usually does the recycling during 4th hour, after he eats second lunch. I take a quick look at my notebook to make sure I have no other plans, and suggest that we have lunch together before we do the recycling. Ananh nods and then asks me if I want to go outside with him during lunch. I say, "Sure. Whatever you want to do is fine with me." He looks at me, raises an eyebrow, and says, "You don't want to know what I do outside." I take this as a hint that he probably smokes, and tell him, "I won't get you in trouble."

For most of the hour, I sit next to Ananh and help him search various Websites for information about Albert Einstein. At one point during this time, I touch his right upper arm and he says, "Ouch!" I apologize and ask why his arm is hurting so much. In his usual way of telling me that he's done something that is prohibited, he says, "You don't want to know." When I reply that I do want to know, he takes his arm out of the sleeve of his sweater, and pulls up the sleeve of the white undershirt. This reveals a large tattoo of the word "JOY," positioned vertically down his arm. I gasp when I see the dry, blue-black tattoo that looks like it may be swollen from inflammation. Ananh ignores my reaction and shares that "Joy" is his nickname, which means "skinny" in Lao. I smile at the simultaneous incongruity and appropriateness of the nickname for such a large, tough-looking, unsmiling young man whom I knew to be gentle and funny. Ananh explains to me that he got the homemade tattoo 3 days ago on a Friday night, from his "homey," a "Viet" 21-year-old guy.

When I voice worries that the tattoo is bruised, peeling, and the skin around it is pink, Ananh shrugs his shoulders and tells me that it just itches but will be fine. He then calls over to Zer and Kia and asks them for lotion. They tell him they don't have any, to which he responds with a scowl punctuated with "Stupid!" I ask Ananh what his parents think about his tattoo and he tells me, "They know. They don't care." But then he adds that this isn't his first tattoo, and he doesn't tell his parents until afterward. He then pulls up the sleeve of the white shirt again, this time to show me a smaller tattoo on the shoulder of the same arm. He explains that a friend also gave him this first one, 3 years ago when he was 14. When I ask him if anything was used to help with the pain, Ananh says, "No. It don't hurt much." I say "Wow" and shake my head at his bravado. Ananh then suggests that I also get a tattoo. I respond with a laugh and tell him that I don't like pain, so I could never do it. Ananh laughs with me, becomes quiet for a brief moment, and then declares that people are "stupid" because they think that if you get a tattoo, you're a "bad person" and "into gangs."

My work with Lao American students such as Ananh illuminated for me the numerous ways our dominant discourses judge, limit, and fix the identities of urban, immigrant students. As Ananh insightfully notes our tendency to invoke vilifying storylines (e.g., of delinquency and gang involvement) to make sense of what it means to be an urban adolescent with a tattoo, he also gestures toward the need for multiple, alternative readings. The words and experiences of Ananh and other Lao students push us to move beyond simplistic, definitive narratives to understand who they are as adolescents, immigrants, and human beings.

Critically, our discourses about students play a vital role in framing how students, teachers, parents, and the general public think about students and schools and their respective responsibilities in educational outcomes. As Wendy Luttrell (2003) persuasively explains, educational

> discourses influence what we take to be true or right or good about ourselves and identities as learners and teachers. There are specific educational discourses that direct our thinking about what it means to be a "problem"—and that characterize as "slow" and "fast," "bright" and "dull," "promising" and "unpromising," or . . . "regular" or "special needs" students. (p. 173).

Problematically, these binary, cohesive discourses provide emphatic declarations about the potential and worthiness of students and families for academic achievement. As with all discourses, these educational narratives position students and families within specific power relations, and prompt us to attend to certain issues but ignore others. Storylines that position students as "special needs" or "promising" influence our expectations and practices as educators and policymakers. Likewise, the portrayal of urban, immigrant families as "traditional" or "dysfunctional" has implications for the types of services and assistance we make available to students and parents. As Davies (2000) suggests, the task of unsettling dominant discourses is "also one of the discovering what the 'hooks' are in the images and metaphors of the old storylines that can draw [us] in against [our] better judgment" (p. 81). We saw Dynamic High teachers and staff drawn in by familiar accounts of unstable homes and urban war zones to imagine and make sense of the lives of their students. We see these "hooks" in news stories about "traditional" cultural practices and the "clash" between the cultures of immigrant families and U.S. society.

Lao American students are trying to figure out and imagine how to exist in the world, producing identities that are ambiguous and conflictual. The incommensurability of their identities resists resolution, refusing to be accommodated within discourses of a singular student identity or even within discourses of plural identities. Thinking and speaking about urban, immigrant students in new ways requires us to shift from an emphasis on the duality of immigrant identity toward an understanding of ambivalent, incongruous—unresolved—identities. Understanding identity as unresolved compels us to transcend the dichotomy of immigrant culture versus U.S. culture, toward what Yon (2000) calls an "elusive culture." It is only in this space that we can acknowledge the experiences of urban, immigrant students, where the contradictions and incompleteness of identity are possible and paramount.

Undercutting the Inside/Outside Opposition

Not quite the Same, not quite the Other, she stands in that unde-termined threshold place where she constantly drifts in and out. Undercutting the inside/outside opposition, her intervention is necessarily that of both a deceptive insider and a deceptive outsider. She is this Inappropriate Other/Same who moves about with always at least two/four gestures: that of affirming "I am like you" while persisting in her difference; and that of reminding "I am different" while unsettling every definition of otherness arrived at.

—Trinh T. Minh-ha, *When the Moon Waxes Red*

Similar to many of the Lao American students at Dynamic High, I am also a refugee from Southeast Asia. My family and I are "boat people," refugees of the Vietnam War. My parents left friends and family and escaped communist Vietnam in search of a better life—the "American Dream"—in the United States. They endured weeks at sea on an overcrowded fishing boat, living through pirates who looted their possessions and raped and kidnapped young female passengers around them. They survived 8 months in an Indonesian refugee camp, overcoming malnutrition and a life-threatening miscarriage. Once in the United States, they started over, swallowing pride to provide for my brothers, sisters, and me; struggling to raise us in a country with unfamiliar norms and expectations. I remember the noisy arguments my sisters and I had with our parents about expected, "appropriate" clothes and behaviors for females. I can hear their exhortations for us to do well in school. I can also recall their struggles with blatant and subtle acts of racism, maintaining public composure while fuming and hurting in the privacy of our home.

This ethnographic study with Lao immigrant students at Dynamic High School was infused with these memories and the histories, politics, standpoints, and contradictions that make up my life (Fine, 1994a). In my research with Lao American students I was at once a researcher, co-constructor of student stories, critical theorist, and immigrant struggling alongside the students. As feminist researchers have convincingly argued, as a social process, qualitative research engages the full complexities of identity work. Discursively constituted, the relationship between researchers and participants, like all social relations, cannot be reduced to binary oppositions of objective/subjective, researcher/ researched, exploiter/exploited, insider/outsider, or student/teacher. In the ambivalence of identity, the boundary between Self and Other are blurred by multiple and conflicting histories, discourses, and power relations. In my research at Dynamic High my subject position necessarily shifted between that of researcher, confidante, immigrant, adult, female, and counselor, among others.

The Social Relations of Research

For the first month and a half of my research at Dynamic High the students did not know what to make of me. Because of my young appearance, many of the students thought I was a new student at the school, whether I was in a 9th grade class or 12th grade class. When I explained to them that I was not a high school student but a university graduate student conducting research at the school, they generally expressed surprise and disbelief. More often than not, they commented on my young appearance and asked, "Are you serious?" Additionally, because many of the students also did not understand what a "graduate" student was, I had to explain the differences between going to college as a graduate student and going as an undergraduate. Without exception, the students did not realize that for certain careers, more than 4 years of college was necessary. When I shared that I had already completed 7 years of postsecondary education, the students replied with "That's a long time to be in school" or "You must be really smart." In turn, I told the students that the time goes by quickly and encouraged them to pursue their career goals, regardless of how long it takes to achieve them. But perhaps more than anything, when I shared that I wanted to learn about their experiences, the students were surprised that anyone would want to take the time to learn about their everyday lives. For the Lao American students who felt ignored in general and at Dynamic in particular, they were simultaneously skeptical that their experiences were worthy of attention and glad that I was interested in their mundane school and life routines.

As is the case with most ethnographic research, it took a little time (about a month and a half) for the students to get used to having me around. As we got to know each other more, the students allowed me into various aspects of their private and academic life. They shared thoughts about teachers and crushes they had on other students, as well as stories about illicit and painfully personal experiences. Somkiat, for example, confided to me that he was gay. He related the disapproval of his parents as well as his experiences as a closeted and ostracized gay student at Dynamic. Speaking about his harassment at school, Somkiat shared the pain of his alienation in this way:

> *Somkiat*: Other students every day, every day they make fun of me and stuff. They call me gay and faggot and stuff. And, when I'm in class people, guys don't want to sit by me because they think I'm going to touch them and whatever. When I'm late for class, I really don't want to go in because I'm scared when I walk in they'll make fun of me. They always do that. My teacher, she sees it too. She always talks to me after class is up.

While teachers supported Somkiat by sending students who made homophobic remarks to the Dean's Office or by comforting him after class, this was not enough to allay his fears and isolation. As he put it, "I feel like there's nobody there to protect me." As we saw in Chapter 1, Somkiat frequently wanted me to go to class with him—perhaps my presence somehow comforted him. On occasions such as the ones I had with Somkiat (and as I illustrate below), I felt that the students wanted and needed a safe space to share stories that they could not otherwise discuss with family or friends. Speaking about her research with high school students, Eckert (1989) notes that she "was not prepared for . . . the number of adolescents who desperately need an adult to talk to" (p. 34). In the same vein, my work at Dynamic High revealed to me that having a sympathetic adult listener who will keep information in confidence was an uncommon opportunity for students.

Stacey (1988) suggests that the appearance that the ethnographic method fosters more connectedness than "traditional" methods may very well mask a more dangerous form of exploitation. According to Stacey, it is "[p]recisely because ethnographic research depends upon human relationship, engagement and attachment, [that] it places research subjects at grave risk of manipulation and betrayal by the ethnographer" (pp. 22–23). With this critique in mind, I worked to remind student participants that I was a researcher, at the school to collect and document their experiences and stories for research purposes. I did this in various ways, from taking out my notebook to jot notes while they spoke, referring to my position as a researcher during the conversation, to asking if they wanted me to include the information in my research. Despite these efforts, students were not deterred from sharing their stories and lives with me. As I discuss below, while I positioned my identity as a "researcher" at the school, the students positioned me in various other ways for their own purposes.

In other ways, students included me in their lives by allowing me to witness or tag along as they engaged in prohibited activities. These activities ranged from passing notes, eating food in class, copying homework, and skipping class to smoking on and off school grounds. As I observed or participated in these illicit activities, the students would sometimes glance at me expectantly, as if they were waiting to see how I would respond. Depending on the occasion, I responded to students by encouraging them to go to class more or with queries such as "Do you know that smoking is bad for you?" Prior to beginning my research, I decided that I did not want to police the behaviors of the students. While I was an adult, I was not at the school to report their mischief to teachers and staff. Indeed, I was not an undercover cop, of the *21 Jump Street* variety, trying to get close to students in order to expose criminal behavior. At the same time, I did not position myself merely as a detached observer who wanted to simply be a "fly on the wall."

About two minutes before the bell, the students pack up and start congregating around the main door to the classroom. Chintana is the only student at the second door. I go to the main door, where Ananh has positioned himself right in front of it. He and Tou are looking at an exhaust switch with a green light and wondering what would happen if they turn it off. Seeing my curiosity, Ananh tells me to turn off the switch. I say no and laugh at them. Ananh then calls over to Ms. Richardson, "Hey, Ms. Richardson. What's it for?" Ms. Richardson looks up from her desk and laughs and tells him that it's just for the exhaust. Ananh asks if he can turn it off and she tells him "Yes." When he flips the switch, the fan stops. He frowns, flips the switch back on and then says, "That's gay." I look at him with a quizzical look on my face and ask, "Why is that gay?" Tou and the other students around us burst into laughter. I realize that they're laughing at Ananh. Tou says, "He says that all of the time." Continuing, Tou tells me that Ananh uses "gay"

*to describe everything and that he "uses it for 'stupid.' " Ananh
adds, "Or dumb."* (FN 9/25/01, Chemistry 11)

Asking Ananh to explain his use of "gay" was not an easy—indeed, it
was even unwise—choice for me. At the time, we were only in the first
few weeks of school, and I did not know Ananh very well. Similar to
the students who laughed at him, Ananh could have understood my
question as a reprimand and chosen to not participate in my study.
It was important for me, however, to ask discomforting questions. To
insist on maintaining the discrete, unitary identity of a "researcher"
who was in the field to be a "distant observer" would have perpetuated
the homophobic norms of school and society (see, e.g., Letts & Sears,
1999; Ngo, 2003). Further, I asked students questions such as "Why is
that gay?" because I wanted to hear their rationale as well as give them
pause to think about their words. In my research at Dynamic, I sought
to refrain from passing judgment on student behaviors and, instead,
worked to create interactions where we could talk about the meanings,
motivations and consequences of their actions (cf. Roman, 1993).

The process of being open to student actions and the ways they
were navigating what it means to be urban, immigrant youth was far
from easy, entangled with my own doubts and uncertainties. While it
was a privilege to be allowed into the multiple dimensions of their
lives, at times it was also exceptionally discomforting. In some instances,
students shared troubling stories about themselves and other students
where choices for action were not apparent, creating persistent echoes
and aches in my head (Fine & Weis, 1998) about what to do or what
I should have done. During lunch one day, for example, Phongsava
told me about a party that she attended over the weekend. When I
asked her if there were Lao students from Dynamic at the party, she
named Ladda. Although I did not know Ladda well, I knew that she
was Trina's younger sister. Just in her first year of high school, I knew
that Ladda had already missed at least 3 weeks of the first semester.
Phongsava continued, declaring that she did not like Ladda because
she was "dirty" or "slept around a lot." According to Phongsava, she
even heard that Ladda "got lined out by the Lao Boys" (a prominent
Lao gang). When I asked what "lined out" meant, she laughed at my
naiveté and then explained that it is when members of a gang line
up to have sex with a girl one after another. As I reacted with distress
to this information—perhaps just gossip—Phongsava merely shrugged
her shoulders and went on to tell another disparaging story about
Ladda.

As I planned for my research at Dynamic, I prepared to report information about physical or sexual abuse of students by other adults by reading the district policy regarding the mistreatment of minors. This proved to be unhelpful, however, because the policy focused on abuse of minors by parents or guardians, and thus did not offer guidelines for the complexity of choices that students made as individuals. Stories like the one about Ladda that students shared that dealt with underage sex, underage drinking, who to go to for marijuana, plans to fight certain students, and going to dance clubs with fake IDs eluded straightforward answers for action. The boundaries of my identity and responsibilities as an "adult" and "researcher" who was yet not a school staff member (or an undercover cop) were unsettled and precarious in the social relations of research. While I was an "adult" and thus "the same" as school teachers and staff, my identity was also persistently different.

More complicated, I found that the students at Dynamic High School were not just "kids" but were also knowledgeable, worldly, savvy, and agents in their own right. Despite my status as an adult and official role as a researcher at the school, I was not always in a privileged position of knowledge and power in relation to the students. Some interactions that I had with the male students, for example, made apparent to me the instability of discrete categories of my identities as adult, researcher, and woman. On a few occasions, these students deliberately flirted with me, making me acutely aware of my gender and sexuality. For instance, I was sitting in Ms. Anderson's advanced ELL class one day, waiting for class to begin. Marcus, a Liberian immigrant student, looked and me and then said to Alexander, another Liberian immigrant student, "She's beautiful." Alexander then looked at me and nodded in agreement. When I asked Alexander if he enjoyed the Sweethearts Dance, he replied that he did because he danced with "a Hmong girl who was cute." As he said this, he stood up and gyrated his hips a little to show me how they danced. Alexander and Marcus shared a laugh together, and then Marcus somberly informed me that he did not attend the dance since he did not have a date. As he explained with a glint in his eyes, this was my fault because he was going to ask me to the dance but I was not around. On another occasion in the same class, Marcus was flirting with me so blatantly that Ms. Anderson even noticed. From the front of the classroom, she jokingly scolded him by saying, "Quit macking on Bic." As the class burst into laughter, I laughed along while marveling at the overt sexuality and boldness of students like Marcus.

Even though students like Marcus and Alexander knew from previous conversations that I was a researcher and several years older, my identities as a researcher and an adult were neither definitive nor cohesive. For some male students, the multiplicity and instability of identity opened up identificatory sites for my positioning as a gendered subject available for sexual advances. For other students, the ambivalence and social relations of identity fostered interactions that positioned me in roles comparable to a mentor, confidante, and friend. Indeed, during the course of my research at Dynamic High I developed close relationships with students as well as teachers. While I was always aware that my role at the school was foremost as a researcher, by the end of my study I had developed close relationships with some teachers and students. I was especially fond of a few students, and cared about how well they did in school, their socioeconomic struggles, and their general well-being. In the next section, I unsettle notions of a cohesive, discrete researcher identity with two fieldnote snapshots of my interactions and conversations with Lao participants Souphattra, Lori, and Nikhong.

Blurred Boundaries

Researcher-Confidante-Friend

I'm sitting with Souphattra in Ceramics again today. We're sitting across from Kia and two other Hmong girls. Eight other girls and three boys are also in the class, sitting a little farther away. Once again, the two long work tables are strewn with plastic bags of clay, scrap pieces of paper, dry clay, and various clay projects. Mr. Sealy is at the wheel again, working on bowls and mugs to sell. Zander is by Mr. Sealy's desk working on his own project. Most of the students are sitting in pairs or small groups talking quietly while they work on their clay pyramids project. Souphattra is more reserved today, almost sad. I can't tell if she wants to talk to me and wonder why she wanted me to come to class with her. I decide to ask what she's planning to do this weekend, to which Souphattra replies, "Nothing. I just watch TV. TV and Thai movies." Knowing that Souphattra and Zander [her boyfriend] are inseparable at school, I ask, "Do you see Zander?" Souphattra responds with "No. Just in school." I then ask, "What do your parents think of Zander?" This question brings Souphattra out of her reticence, and she tells me, "They think he's okay. They don't want me to be with or marry a White guy. They want me to marry an Asian guy. Any Asian guy. But I can't marry before I get an education and a job." I ask if other Lao parents feel that way about daughters getting an education and Souphattra says, "No. Most parents don't care about their children like my parents." She further explains that for some girls, their parents force them to marry because they worry the girls are going to get in trouble [have sex]. "They marry them off before they can do anything." As she continues more slowly, Souphattra tells me that this is okay, because she's "not going to end up with Zander." I see that she is definitely sad now, and I hesitantly ask, "Why do you think you won't be together?" Souphattra shrugs her shoulders, looks at me, and then looks down again at the clay and says, "He's told me that he doesn't like me as much." I could only respond with "I'm so sorry." Once again, Souphattra shrugs her shoulders and then tells me, "I'm trying to get over it before I break up with him." She continues to tell me that Zander is her first boyfriend and that when they first started dating in the 10th grade he would "do anything" to keep her. Souphattra gives me an example by sharing that Zander used to do a lot of drugs but then quit because she didn't like it. Now, Zander thinks "he's always right and tries to tell me what to do."

I catch up with Souphattra outside of her math class today. We stop at her locker so that she can exchange books for the classes she has after lunch. I see that Zander is nowhere in sight and ask about him. Souphattra tells me that he's probably already downstairs in line to get lunch. On our way to the cafeteria I ask if she and Zander are planning to go to the Sweethearts Dance this weekend. She tells me "probably not" and asks, "Are you going?" I say "Yes," but then worry that Souphattra might be sad about not going. I then add that she and Zander could go to Prom together. After a brief pause, she says, "Probably not." A little surprised, I ask, "Why?" Once more, Souphattra gives me a short answer and says, "Zander doesn't want to go with me." A little alarmed now, I ask, "Why doesn't he want to go with you?" Souphattra slows down her pace, glances at me, and then says, "We broke up 3 weeks ago." Taken aback by the news, I say to Souphattra, "I'm so surprised. I'm so sorry." By this time, we are in the cafeteria and sit down at the first empty table. I tell her that we don't have to talk about the breakup if she doesn't want to. Souphattra tells me "It's okay" and then shares that it started when she asked Zander how he felt about her. He told her that he didn't feel the same way about her as he used to, and that he didn't love her. She decided to break up with him because she didn't want to be with someone who doesn't love her. Souphattra continues to share that she is still sad sometimes about it, because she still cares about him. It's also hard and confusing because Zander is still affectionate and gives her hugs and kisses. She ends the explanation by stating, "I don't know how to feel when he does this." Seeing her despair, I try to comfort Souphattra by sharing my experience with breakups, pointing out that my sadness and hurt got better over time. When I finish, we both sit quietly for about a minute. I then suggest we get our lunches and Souphattra agrees. We get up from the table and make our way to the lunch line. We stand together for a few minutes without talking, inching forward as the line moves. Unexpectedly, Souphattra breaks the silence and asks, "Do you want to go for pho [Vietnamese noodle soup] this weekend?"

Researcher-Mentor-Friend

After I get to school, I decide to go to Ms. Randall's first hour to see what Nikhong, Vonechai, and Xay were up to for the day. The bell just rang, so I slip into the class quietly and sit down next to Nikhong. Nikhong has her *Issues Day* schedule out and hands it to me when I gesture at it. I see that she's signed up for "Reality Check: Things teens should know before leaving home," *Hoop Dreams*, and "Fun with Chemistry." Nikhong whispers that Lori will be in the "Reality Check" workshop with her. I also glance at Xay's schedule and learn that he's signed up for several things about dance and hip-hop. Vonechai is scheduled to be in a criminal law workshop as well as a workshop on racism. I decide to follow Nikhong to her first workshop.

When the bell rings, we head to her locker. On our way down the stairs, Nikhong makes a comment about how the particular stairway is always crowded from the basement to the third floor. She continues to tell me that she "hates it when people line up in the middle of the hall to just talk" or when they walk really slowly. We reach her locker and Nikhong turns the combination lock, but it doesn't open. She tries again, and once again it doesn't open. I ask Nikhong if she has the correct locker. We both look at the number on the locker and she tells me that it's the right one. As Nikhong tries the combination again, Lori walks up and asks us what we're doing, and I explain that Nikhong can't get her locker open. For a third time, the locker doesn't open for Nikhong, and she says, "Forget it" and is ready to leave. I tell her I want to try and dial the numbers as Nikhong tells them to me. Happily, it opens and we exclaim "Alright!" As we walk to the "Reality Check" workshop, Lori and I tease Nikhong for not be able to open her own locker. We turn down the main hall into a mass of students, and shift from walking side-by-side to walking in single file.

As we make our way through the students, Nikhong and Lori both turn back toward me a few times to look at me, as if to make sure I am still with them. This makes me smile.

. . . A white man in his mid-thirties from Project Solo is leading the class in the "Reality Check" workshop. He explains to the mostly female group of 22 students that his organization works with homeless youth. He tells us that he plans to talk about some of the issues that youth face after leaving home to try to live on their own. He asks the class to get into five groups and then gives us a list of questions to consider. These "living on your own" questions include: "How much does an apartment cost?" and "Where do I find an apartment?" . . . Nikhong and Lori, who are sitting next to each other opposite me, keep looking at me and mouth, "This is boring." Lori takes out a piece of notebook paper and starts to doodle on it, spelling and decorating her name and my name with flowers, stars and curly cues. . . . One question that was especially interesting to Lori, Nikhong, and Zer included "When would be a good age to move out of your parent's house?" Nikhong tells the group that 18 is an ideal age, while Lori suggests "Twenty-one." Nikhong then adds with emphasis, "I can't wait until I'm 18." According to Nikhong, her mom has told her that when she turns 18, she can do whatever she wants. She's anxious to have more freedom and be free of babysitting responsibilities. I remind Lori and Nikhong that they're both planning to go to college, so they wouldn't be living on their own for a while. They laugh and say, "Oh yeah." Lori then asks me, "What's it like living alone?" I tell them that this is the first year that I have lived in a place by myself. I share my initial worries that I would feel lonely, but that things turned out well because I love having my own space. As I continue to tell the girls about my general experience living alone, including my mom's fears, they listen intently and nod their heads. After I finish, Lori simply smiles at me. Nikhong remarks, "I couldn't live alone. I need company" and gets a laugh from all of us.

The Inadequacy of Categories

During my research I developed relationships with students like Souphattra, Lori, and Nikhong where we engaged with each other as human beings, sharing moments of silliness and sadness, as well as hopes and fears. My preparation to "do research" did not prepare me for the intimacy of the heartache of Souphattra's dating relationship, Lori's question about my experiences living alone as a guidepost for her own thinking, or the general appreciation of my presence by the students.

As I try to label my relationship with students like Lori, Nikhong, and Souphattra, I am once again confronted by the inadequacy of our discrete categories for identity. My interactions, conversations and positionings at Dynamic High cannot be described by stable, cohesive categories of "researcher," "mentor," "confidante," "adult," or "friend." Indeed, my attempt to name my relationships with the above section subtitles is also unsatisfactory, and rings hollow in my ears. I was all of this and more, something that was "not quite the Same, not quite the Other" (Trinh, 1991, p. 74).

The instability of my researcher identity raises epistemological and methodological questions of research: What are the implications of a research relationship that might be deemed a "friendship?" What are the responsibilities of a researcher when participants want to engage in a mentoring relationship? The response from some feminist ethnographers has problematized notions of "friendship" and intimacy in the social relations of research. These critics argue that the "friendship" role of the adult researcher creates an inauthentic space of safety for vulnerable adolescents who need an adult "sympathetic listener" to share their problems and struggles. As Stacey (1988) puts it, "The lives, loves, and tragedies that fieldwork informants share with a researcher are ultimately data, grist for the ethnographic mill" (p. 23). Similarly, Finch (1984) argues that a research method that encourages intimacy, friendship, and disclosure on the part of the participants to gain data, may very well place participants in positions of (emotional, psychological, and physical) jeopardy. During the course of her research, she found that it was relatively easy to get most women to reveal extremely private aspects of their lives. Finch thus concludes: "I have emerged from interviews with the feeling that my interviewees need to know how to protect themselves from people like me" (p. 80). In the same vein, Cotterill (1992) argues:

> [D]uring the research process, [the researcher] may create expectations which encourage some respondents to make disclosures they would only make to close friends. In an interview situation which seeks to be egalitarian and involves listening with care and concern, the distinction between a research relationship and a friendship may become blurred. And when a woman talks about very painful aspects of her life to another who will eventually walk away, there may be real potential for harm (p. 599).

For Cotterill, a research method that is based on personal interactions and "listening with care and concern" problematically fosters the blurring of a research relationship and friendship.

I suggest that while we need to cling to methodological and epistemological reflexivity and responsibility, we cannot hold on to the unity of an identity as a "researcher" in thinking about our research relationships and positioning in the field. Cotterill's concern that "the distinction between a research relationship and a friendship may be blurred" is in reality a necessary outcome of the discursive relations of identity. The ethical and epistemological concerns surrounding the positioning of the researcher within ethnographic research cannot be reduced simply to notions of an intentional identity that the ethnographer takes up while in the field. Because identity is discursively constituted by ourselves as well as others, how we position ourselves (e.g., as a researcher) and how others position us (e.g., as a friend, confidante) may collide and conflict. Our research participants do not merely exist as pawns, to be easily manipulated for research purposes, but engage with us with their own intentions. While I may want students to engage with me as "participants" in my research, they may choose to engage with me from other subject positions and motivations. Similarly, while I may want to be identified as a researcher and as an adult, my research participants may read me differently. At Dynamic High, I was misrecognized by students, teachers, and staff as a "student," and variously positioned as a researcher, individual of sexual interest, confidante, and mentor, among others. Much like the social relations of identity, in the social relations of ethnographic research, the "real me" of my researcher identity was a site of negotiation and instability. Rather than whole and seamless, the identity of the researcher must be "conceived as dialectical and shifting, operating through multiple and conflicting sets of discourses and power relations" (Roman, 1993, p. 208).

A Note on Methodology

Research Setting

This ethnographic study was conducted from September 2001 to July 2002 in Lakes City, a large, urban city in the Midwestern United States. According to the 2000 U.S. Census, Lakes City had a total population of 382,618. Of the total population 22,963 or 6% of the city population was composed individuals of Asian heritage. The Hmong was the largest Asian ethnic group at 9,595, followed by Vietnamese (2,395), Chinese (2,369), and Lao (2,212). The Midwestern state in which Lakes City is located has the second largest Lao population, next to California.

The Lakes City Public Schools is the largest school district in the state. As the largest school district in an urban center, Lakes City Public Schools had over 11,000 students in the school system that were learning English or spoke another language at home. Over half (67%) of its students lived in poverty. In the year that I conducted my research, students in the district were comprised of African or African American (45%), White American (26%), Asian American (14%), Hispanic American (11%), and Native American (4%). Of these students, 245 were English Language Learners. Sixty-seven percent of the students were eligible for free or reduced lunch.

During the 2001–2002 academic year, the Lakes City Public Schools had 63 elementary schools, 8 middle schools, and 7 high schools. In addition, there were 31 alternative schools and 6 special education schools in the district. These schools were a major component of the district's open enrollment or "Choice" plan, which allowed Lakes City families to choose the schools for their children. This open enrollment gave families who lived in the northern half of Lakes City the opportunity to enroll their children in a northern Lakes City magnet school, north Lakes City community school, or a school from one of 8 suburban school districts to the north and west of the city. Likewise, families who lived in the southern half of the city were able to choose from southern Lakes City magnet schools, southern Lakes City community schools, and a school from four suburban school districts to the west or south of the city.

This "Choice" plan was created as a result of the settlement of lawsuits that were filed by the Lakes City branch of the National Association for the Advancement of Colored People (NAACP) and the Lakes City parents against the state. "Choice" is the product of the collaboration between the NAACP, parents, the state, and Lakes City and suburban school districts. It began in 2001 and was guaranteed to be funded through spring 2005. Students who enrolled in the program may remain in the same (suburban) school district until high school graduation. In order to participate in "Choice" families must submit their application by January 15 for the following fall. Families who participate in "Choice" do not have to pay tuition and transportation is free. Throughout the year—even in the summer—parents may visit Lakes City schools, talk with staff or take a tour to help them determine which school best fits their child. Moreover, most schools hold open houses between November and January and the district holds its annual "Choice" Fair the first Saturday in November. According to Lakes City Public Schools, 98% of incoming kindergarten families who submit their "Choice" application by the January 15 deadline receive their first or second choice. Literature on the "Choice" plan highlight that "Choice" "helps families of all ethnic and racial backgrounds make good choices for their children's education."

The School

The primary site of my research was at Dynamic High School a large, urban, public high school. Dynamic High was one of 7 high schools in Lakes City. Located in a poor to working-class industrial area of the city, the high school enrolled approximately 1,482 students from across the city. The majority of the students in the school were either African or African American (43%), Asian American (mostly Hmong American) (38%), and White American (16%). During the 2001–2002 academic year, 8% of the Asian American students at Dynamic were Lao American. While the socioeconomic status of the students ranged from working-class to middle-class, the majority of the students (75%) qualified for free or reduced lunches.

Staff members at Dynamic included one principal, two assistant principals (one of which was a teacher on special assignment), 29 licensed staff who were not classroom teachers, 59 non-licensed staff, and 85 classroom teachers. Fifty-eight percent of the staff members were female and 42% male. The majority of the staff was White (73%), along with African American (19%), Asian American (4%), Latino American (3%), and Native American (1%). Of the 85 classroom teachers, 66% were tenured (compared to 73% in the district) and 44% had earned a Master's degree or higher (compared to 51% in the district).

The majority of the students at Dynamic High were enrolled in the Comprehensive Program, the lowest academic track at the school. According to school literature, the program provides students with a "traditional" education, with courses in English, math, science, and social studies. Teachers who teach comprehensive courses were part of "teams." This team approach was designed to ensure that Dynamic students are offered an interdisciplinary education, allowing them to make connections across subject areas. In addition to the Comprehensive Program the school houses two magnet programs, including one of two International Baccalaureate (IB) programs in the district and an Open program. The IB Magnet was one of the most prestigious magnets in the school and district. As a pre-college program, it used an internationally-recognized curriculum to help prepare students for college coursework. The other magnet program at Dynamic High was called the Open Magnet, an alternative magnet program that provided students within the large school with a small, structured learning community. According to school literature, the content of the Open Magnet offered core courses such as English, math, social studies, and science; the classes emphasized self-directed, cooperative, interdisciplinary learning. In order to be considered for the IB and Open programs, students were required to complete a district application that included two recommendations from teachers, a graded writing sample, and the transcript of their grades. Applicants to the IB program also needed to have a GPA of 2.5 or better. During the 2001–2002 academic year, 20% of the students in the IB program and 43% of students in the Open program were students of color. Moreover, Dynamic High offered both an English Language Learners (ELL) and a bilingual program. This program provided students who were learning English as a second language with ELL classes. For the Hmong American ELL students at the school, some classes were also offered in Hmong. Lastly, Dynamic had a special education program for students with emotional or behavioral disabilities.

Negotiating Entry

During the spring of 2001, I identified two cities in the Midwestern United States with a large Asian American population. I contacted the research and evaluation departments for the school districts in the metropolitan area and asked them to provide me with demographic information for the students in the high schools. I analyzed the student information, focusing on schools with the largest Lao American student population, Asian American population, and general student racial and ethnic diversity. I also conducted research on the different schools, looking at information available on district Websites. I paid special attention to schools with a range of academic programs, including advanced placement and ELL programs.

From my analysis of the school data, I narrowed my choices for a research setting to two high schools from the Lakes City Public Schools. I contacted the district and asked for the guidelines for applying to conduct research in the district. The district sent me an application packet, which required me to detail the research question, research design, human subjects protocol, and my rationale for choosing the school district. I was also informed that the school's principal would have final say in whether or not I may conduct research at the school. I contacted the school secretary for both high schools and made appointments to meet with the principals. After meeting with both principals, I chose Dynamic High School for my research site. In large part, this was due to the fact that it had the largest Lao American student population in the school district. I wanted to focus on Lao students because of the dearth of research on this particular group of students. Moreover, Dynamic was of particular interest, because of the racial, ethnic, and economic diversity of the student body as well as the school's reputation for being a great place for students as well as teachers.

Data Collection and Analysis

As I mentioned previously, the data collection for this study took place from September 2001 through July 2002. During this time period I spent four to five days a week at Dynamic High observing students and teachers inside and outside of the classroom and participating in various school activities. I attended school dances (e.g., Prom), club meetings (e.g., Asian Culture Club), sports games, and graduation. I also was involved in more informal school activities such as hanging out with students during lunch, in the hallways, in the library, outside in front of the school, and in the women's restrooms. Additionally, upon the request of two teachers, I also helped chaperone two school field trips (one to an art museum and the other to a festival of nations event). Moreover, I participated in several community events with students, including going to parks, church, and family ceremonial services with the Lao American student participants. These participant-observations focused on the ways in which students, teachers, and school staff understood and talked about culture and cultural difference, with special attention to the experiences and interactions with Lao American students. These observations allowed me to note the interactions of Lao American students with teachers, staff, and students. In turn, these observations of interactions allowed me to triangulate the remarks made by participants in informal conversations and interviews. During this fieldwork, I also collected documents such as daily announcements, school and community newspapers, yearbooks, class handouts, and event fliers.

After a few months of fieldwork, I focused my participant-observations on certain students and teachers who were especially helpful and interesting for my research purposes. These primary participants included 7 focal Lao American students and 4 focal teachers. In addition, I interviewed and observed 30 other Lao American students, their Hmong American and White American peers, teachers, and school staff. The Lao students who participated in my study were all 1.5- or second-generation immigrants. In other words, these students either came to the United States when they were still very young (1.5-generation) or were born in the United States (second-generation). The Lao students came from poor, blue-collar families. Their parents were employed in various factories, and many of the students worked jobs to support their families or themselves. The students lived in neighborhoods close to the school that many characterized as "ghetto." All of the students received free or reduced lunches. Lao students who appear in this book include Ananh, Chintana, Kett, Lori, Mindy, Nikhong, Phongsava, Somkiat, Sompong, Souphattra, and Vonechai. Teachers and staff include Ms. Anderson, Ms. Evans, Ms. Gates, Mr. Gibson, Ms. Hanson, Ms. Jenkins, Ms. Kane, Ms. Perry, Mr. Rogers, Ms. Sanders, and Mr. Sullivan.

I conducted audiotaped, semi-structured, open-ended interviews with 41 Lao American students, their peers, and school faculty and staff. The interviews focused on (1) The perceptions and experiences of Lao American students with their peers and teachers; (2) The family life of Lao students; and (3) The perceptions and experiences of school students, teachers, and staff with Lao American students. These interviews often took place after school in the library, in empty classrooms, or in the homes of the students. On average, each of the interviews and follow-up interviews for each participant lasted a little over an hour.

The interviews were audiotaped and transcribed. The interview transcripts as well as the fieldnotes from participant-observations were coded and analyzed in two different phases. First, I open coded the data line-by-line to identify and create possible ideas, themes, or issues that the data might suggest (Bogdan & Biklen 1992; Miles & Huberman 1994; Strauss & Corbin 1998). In the second phase of coding and analysis, I engaged in focused coding, where I analyzed and organized the data line-by-line, using specific topics that I identified as especially of interest (Bogdan & Biklen 1992; Wolcott 1994). This smaller set of ideas provided the major topics and themes for deeper analysis and for writing the larger study. While this analytic approach draws extensively from "grounded theory," it also differs from it in that I understand that research data do not stand alone, but that my analysis pervades all stages of my research project.

Notes

Chapter 1

1. The names of people and places are pseudonyms.

2. There are several studies that examine the experiences of Asian American and other immigrant groups. These studies generally emphasize culture and the experiences of an Asian American immigrant group from a historical perspective. My work approaches culture from a poststructuralist perspective and provides an alternative lens for thinking about the cultures of ethnic groups.

3. See Appendix B for an explication of the methodology.

4. I explain in detail my identity as a researcher in Appendix A.

5. Once a year, Dynamic High teachers and staff organized an *Issues Day*, which was initiated by Andrew Flowers, a prominent leader from the Lakes City community. On a few visits to the school in the early 1990s, Mr. Flowers saw female students sexually assaulted, pregnant female students harassed, racism and racial tension, violence among the Blood and Crip gang members, and a gay male student forced to strip in a boy's bathroom. Deeply troubled by what he witnessed at the school, Flowers organized leaders from various community organizations to come to Dynamic High to discuss issues that were important to students in their everyday lives. On *Issues Day* instead of going to regularly scheduled classes, students signed up for sessions that addressed various social and economic issues. While parents had the option to excuse their children from school on *Issues Day*, several teachers shared that the number of complaints from parents has markedly decreased since its inception. The 2001–2002 *Issues Day* was organized by a small group of students and teachers, who worked for a period of several months to solicit input from teachers and students and schedule speakers from various community organizations. The schedule of the sessions was extensive and spanned a range of topics. Movies that were offered included *Gandhi, Princess Mononoki, Finding Forrester, The Joy Luck Club, Hoop Dreams,* and *Crouching Tiger, Hidden Dragon*. Other sessions addressed concerns from homelessness to credit card debt to eating disorders.

6. The Lao American students who appear in this study include Ananh, Chintana, Kett, Lori, Mindy, Nikhong, Phongsava, Somkiat, Sompong, Souphattra, Trina, and Vonechai.

Chapter 2

1. The year of my research at Dynamic High was only the second year that the school had a student council.

2. Dynamic High School was home to a teacher-mentoring program, the Professional Practice School (PPS), which was a collaboration between the teachers' union and the major state university. It was the only professional practice school in the district and state. The program mentored teachers through the different stages of their careers and made the education of teachers and teaching a reflective, ongoing process. The PPS offered professional development opportunities to teachers, including practicum and student teaching experiences for pre-service teachers; a residency program for new teachers; support for teachers to obtain tenure; staff forums, professional development cohorts, and action research groups for all teachers; mentoring for National Board Certification cohorts; guest lecture opportunities for teachers with Master's degrees; and a Leadership Institute for teacher leaders and administrators.

3. To protect the anonymity of the school, I want to note that this is not necessarily the geographic area of the city in which the school was located.

4. Dynamic High had one of two International Baccalaureate (IB) programs in the Lakes City Public Schools. The IB magnet was one of the most prestigious magnets in the school and district. It is a challenging pre-college program that used an internationally recognized curriculum that provides students with 4 years of pre-college courses. In order to be considered for IB, students must have a GPA of 2.5 or better and complete a district application that included two recommendations from teachers, a graded writing sample, and transcript of grades. Students from across the city were eligible (and did) apply to the program. During the 2001–2002 academic year only 20% of the students in the IB program were students of color.

5. Students qualified for free or reduced lunch if their family income was at or below the poverty line. For example, according to district income guidelines, a family of five with a yearly income of $38,240 would qualify for free/reduced lunch. During the 2001–2002 school year, the cost for breakfast at Dynamic and other secondary schools was $1.10 and the cost of lunch was $1.60. The reduced prices were $.30 for breakfast and $.40 for lunch. The number of students who qualified for reduced lunch at Dynamic was 75%, compared to the District average of 58%.

6. Similar to the teachers and staff, the students at Dynamic also remarked on the diversity of the school and that it was not as violent or bad as others. For example, according to Nikhong, Dynamic was not "too ghetto" or the best or the worst school: "It's a good school to go to. It's not too ghetto. Like the bathrooms have locks and the teachers are pretty good. There's not a lot of mean teachers and stuff. I mean Dynamic's an average school. It's not the best or the worst." As a way to describe the school, students also talked about the diversity of the racial, ethnic, and class backgrounds of the student population. Nikhong called it a "big mix of culture." "I think it's a big mix of culture. Like

there's Laos, there's Cambodian, there's Hmong, there's Black, there's White. But the majority is of course Black and Hmong. There's still a mix. Like in the classrooms you'll see a mix of people not only White or not only Black." Importantly, students also noted the ways students segregated themselves along racial, ethnic, or class lines. For example, Vonechai shared: "Dynamic is very diverse. It's a high school that is in a way open to everyone, but also closed. Because of the fact that there are so many people in the school you tend to kind of get segregated off into either race, class, financial well-being, or some kind of common ground. And it seems like the common ground that's mostly seen is race. Like it is in a way segregated off by race."

Chapter 3

1. See Appendix B for an explanation of the academic programs at Dynamic High School.

Chapter 4

1. Additionally, the U.S. Bureau of the Census included smaller Asian American groups within the category of "All Other Asians" in the 1980 Census: Bangladeshi, Bhutanese, Bornean, Burmese, Celbesian, Cernan, Indochinese, Iwo-Jiman, Javanese, Malayan, Maldivian, Nepali, Okinawan, Sikkimese, Singaporean, and Sri Lankan (Pang, 1990).

2. The frequent identification of Asian Americans as Chinese or Japanese may be due to the fact that they are two of the oldest and most established Asian ethnic groups in the United States; and because the familiarity with these two groups is due to our domestic and foreign policies toward Chinese and Japanese immigrants in the U.S. and the Chinese and Japanese governments (see, e.g., Kitano and Daniels 1995; Takaki 1989).

3. The "confusion" stemmed from a debate that the Asian Club was really a Hmong Club because it was dominated by Hmong American students and excluded students from other Asian ethnic groups. I address this later in the book.

4. Toua prepared this statement on a piece of paper and read directly from it. I asked for the paper after the show.

Chapter 5

1. I want to note that Ms. Perry's comparison of African American and Lao American students with different breeds of dogs is problematic. For the purposes of this chapter, I will not unpack the comment further, except to say that this comment is inconsistent with Ms. Perry's concern for students and

work against issues of racism and sexism in the school and society. I return
to discuss this contradiction in Chapter 6.

2. Students earned different awards for their academic achievements each
quarter. This included (a) 4.0 Grade Point Average (GPA) and up: Subway
coupon; (b) 3.6667 GPA and up: A Honor Roll, t-shirt with name on back,
certificate, and gold card for discounts (e.g., Sam Goody); and (c) 2.6667 and
up: B Honor Roll, t-shirt, certificate, and silver card. In addition, students
were also rewarded for GPA improvements and school attendance. The awards
included (a).5 GPA and up improvement per quarter: t-shirt, certificate, red
card; (b) Perfect Attendance: $75 savings bond for no absences in all classes
except school-related activities; and (c) Excellent Attendance: free movie
pass/coupon for no more than four absences for all classes.

References

Abrams, J. (2007 September 25). Congress examines hip-hop language. *USA Today.* on October 1, 2007 from http://www.usatoday.com/life/music/news/2007-09-25-hip-hop-congress_N.htm.

Anderson, E. (1999). *Code of the street: Decency, violence and the moral life of the inner city.* New York: Norton.

Anyon, J. (1997). *Ghetto schooling: A political economy of urban educational reform.* New York: Teachers College Press.

Anzaldua, G. (1987). *Borderlands—La frontera: The new mestiza.* San Francisco: Aunt Lute.

Apple, M. (2000). *Official knowledge: Democratic education in a conservative age.* New York: Routledge.

Banks, J. A. (1995). Multicultural education: Historical developments, dimensions and practice. In J. A. Banks, & C. M. Banks (Eds.), *Handbook of research on multicultural education* (pp. 3–34). New York: Macmillan.

Bennett, C. (2001). Genres of research in multicultural education. *Review of Educational Research, 71*(2), 171–217.

Bhabha, H. (1990). The third space: Interview with Homi Bhabha. In J. Rutherford (Ed.), *Identity: Community, culture, difference* (pp. 207–221). London: Lawrence and Wishart.

Bhabha, H. (1994). *The location of culture.* New York: Routledge.

Bhabha, H. (1999). Staging the politics of difference: Homi Bhabha's Critical Literacy. Interview with Gary Olson and Lynn Worsham. In G. Olson, & L. Worsham (Eds.), *Race, rhetoric and the postcolonial* (pp. 3–39). Albany, New York: SUNY.

Bogdan, R. C., & Biklen, S. K. (1992). *Qualitative research for education: An introduction to theory and methods.* Boston: Allyn & Bacon.

Brandt, S. (2007 February 26). Four beat the odds and will soon be off to college. *Star Tribune,* 1B.

Britzman, D. (2000). "The Question of Belief": Writing Poststructural Ethnography. In E. A. St. Pierre, & W. S. Pillow (Eds.), *Working the ruins: Feminist poststructural theory and methods in education* (pp. 27–40). New York: Routledge.

Britzman, D. P. (1998). *Lost subjects, contested objects: Toward a Psychoanalytic Inquiry of Learning.* Albany: State University of New York Press.

Burbules, N. C. (1997). A grammar of difference: Some ways of rethinking difference and diversity as educational topics. *Australian Educational Researcher, 24*(1), 97–116.

Butler, J. (1993). *Bodies that Matter.* New York: Routledge.

Caplan, N., Choy, M. H., & Whitmore, J. K. (1991). *Children of the boat people: A study of educational success.* Ann Arbor, MI: University of Michigan Press.

Chang, J., & Herc, D. J. K. (2005). *Can't stop won't stop: A history of the hip-hop generation.* New York: St. Martin's Press.

Chaudhry, L. N. (2000). Researching "my people," researching myself: Fragments of a reflexive tale. In E. A. St. Pierre, & W. S. Pillow (Eds.), *Working the Ruins: Feminist Poststructuralist Methods in Education* (pp. 96–113). New York: Routledge.

Clifford, J. (1988). *The predicament of culture: Twentieth-Century Ethnography, Literature, and Art.* Cambridge, MA: Harvard University Press.

Clifford, J., & Marcus, G. (Eds.) (1986). *Writing culture: The poetics and politics of ethnography* (pp 1–26). Berkeley, CA: University of California Press.

Corwin, M. (2000). *And still we rise: The trials and triumphs of twelve gifted inner city schools.* New York: Morrow.

Cotterill, P. (1992). Interviewing women: Issues of friendship, vulnerability, and power. *Women's Studies International Forum, 15*(5/6), 593–606.

Davidson, A. L. (1996). *Making and molding identity in schools: Student narratives on race, gender and academic engagement.* NY: SUNY Press.

Davies, B. (1993). *Poststructuralist theory and classroom practice.* Geelong, Vic.: Deakin University Press.

Davies, B. (2000). *A body of writing.* Walnut Creek, CA: AltaMira Press.

Denn, R. (2000 June 8). Schools go to bat for Gates scholarship applicants. *Seattle Post—Intelligencer,* B1.

Do, Anh. (2002). Taking on two worlds. *Orange County Register,* January 11. Retrieved November 15, 2006 from http://www.proquest.umi.com.

Du Bois, W. E. B. (1953). *The souls of Black folk.* New York: Fawcett.

Ellsworth, E. (1989). Why doesn't this feel empowering?: Working through the repressive myths of critical pedagogy. *Harvard Educational Review, 59*(3), 297–324.

Ellsworth, E. (1997). *Teaching positions: Difference, pedagogy, and the power of address.* New York: Teachers College Press.

Ellsworth, E. (2006). *Places of learning: Media, architecture, pedagogy.* New York: RoutledgeFalmer.

Espiritu, Y. L. (1992). *Asian American panethnicity.* Philadelphia: Temple University Press.

Espiritu, Y. L. (2007). *Asian American women and men: Labor, laws, and love.* Lanham, MD: Rowman and Littlefield Publishers, Inc.

Feagans, B. (2006). Generation 1.5: Young immigrants in two worlds. *The Atlanta Journal-Constitution,* September 3. Retrieved November 15, 2006 from http://www.proquest.umi.com.

Finch, J. (1984). It's great to have someone to talk to: The ethics and politics of interviewing women. In H. Roberts and C. Bell (Eds.), *Social Researching: Politics, Problems, Practice* (pp. 70–87). London: Routledge & Kegan Paul.

Fine, M. (1994a). Working the hyphens: Reinventing the Self and Other in qualitative research. In N. R. Denzin, & Y. S. Lincoln (Eds.), *Handbook of Qualitative Research,* 70–82. Thousand Oaks, CA: Sage.

Fine, M. (1994b). Dis-stance and other stances: Negotiations of power inside feminist research. In A. Gitlin (Ed.), *Power and method: Political activism and educational research* (pp. 13–35). New York: Routledge.

Fine, M., & Weis, L. (1998). *The unknown city: Lives of poor and working-class young adults.* Boston: Beacon Press.

Flores-Gonzalez, N. (2005). Popularity versus respect: School structure, peer groups, and Latino academic achievement. *International Journal of Qualitative Studies in Education, 18*(5), 625–642.

Fordham, S. (1993). "Those loud Black girls": Black women, silence, and 'passing' in the academy. *Anthropology and Education Quarterly, 24*(1), 3–32.

Foucault, M. (1979). *Discipline and punish: The birth of the prison.* New York: Vintage.

Foucault, M. (1983). The subject and power. In H. L. Dreyfus, & P. Rabinow (Eds.), *Michel Foucault: Beyond structuralism and hermeneutics* (pp. 208–226). Chicago: University of Chicago Press.

Freire, P. (1973). *Pedagogy of the oppressed.* New York: Seabury Press.

Gee, J. (1996). *Social linguistics and literacies: Ideology and discourses.* 2nd ed. Philadelphia: Falmer Press, Taylor and Francis.

Gilroy, P. (1991). *"There ain't no Black in the union Jack": The cultural politics of race and nation.* Chicago: The University of Chicago Press.

Gitlin, A., Buendia, E., Crosland, K., & Doumbia, F. (2003). The production of margin and center: Welcoming-unwelcoming of immigrant students. *American Educational Research Journal 40*(1), 91–122.

Glesne, C. (2005). *Becoming qualitative researchers.* Boston: Allyn & Bacon.

Goldberg, D. T. (1994). Introduction: Multicultural conditions. In D. T. Goldberg (Ed.), *Multiculturalism: A critical reader* (pp. 1–44). Cambridge, MA: Blackwell.

Gonick, M. (2003). *Between femininities: Ambivalence, identity, and the education of girls.* New York: SUNY Press.

Hall, K. (1995). "There's a time to act English and a time to act Indian": The politics of identity among British-Sikh teenagers. In S. Stephens (Ed.), *Children and the Politics of Culture* (pp. 243–264). Princeton, NJ: Princeton University Press.

Hall, S. (1990). Cultural identity and diaspora. In J. Rutherford (Ed.), *Identity: Community, culture, difference* (pp. 222–239). London: Lawrence and Wishart.

Hall, S. (1996). Introduction: Who needs 'identity'? In S. Hall & P. du Gay (Eds.), *Questions of cultural identity* (pp. 1–17). Thousand Oaks, CA: Sage.

Hall, S., & du Gay, P. (Eds.) (1996). *Questions of cultural identity.* Thousand Oaks, CA: Sage.

Harding, S. (1987). *Feminism and methodology: Social science issues.* Bloomington: Indiana University Press.

Haymes, S. N. (1995). *Race, culture and the city: A pedagogy for Black urban struggle.* Albany: State University of New York Press.

Hemmings, A. (2002). Youth culture of hostility: Discourses of money, respect and difference. *International Journal of Qualitative Studies in Education, 15*(3), 291–307.

hooks, b. (1990). *Yearning: Race, gender and cultural politics.* Boston: South End Press.

hooks, b. (1992). *Black looks: Race and representation.* Boston: South End Press.

Hune, S. (2000). Rethinking race: paradigms and policy formation. In M. Zhou & J.V. Gatewood (Eds.), *Contemporary Asian America: a multidisciplinary reader* (pp. 667–676). New York: New York University Press.

Kelley, T. (2008 March 25). In an era of school shootings, a new drill. *New York Times.* Retrieved on June 6, 2008 from http://www.nytimes.com/2008/03/25/nyregion/25drills.html?_r = 1&oref = slogin.

Kibria, N. (1993). *Family tightrope: The changing lives of Vietnamese Americans.* Princeton, NJ: Princeton University Press.

Kitano, H., & Daniels, R. (1995). *Asian-Americans: Emerging minorities.* Englewood, NJ: Prentice-Hall.

Kondo, D. (1990). *Crafting selves: Power, gender and discourses of identity in a Japanese workplace.* Chicago: University of Chicago Press.

Kozol, J. (1991). *Savage inequalities: Children in America's schools.* New York: HarperPerrennial.

Krulfeld, R. M. (1994). Buddhism, maintenance, and change: Reinterpreting gender in a Lao refugee community. In L. A. Camino, & R. M. Krulfeld (Eds.), *Reconstructing lives, recapturing meaning: Refugee identity, gender, and culture change* (pp. 97–127). Amsterdam, Netherlands: Gordon and Breach Publishers.

Kumashiro, K. (1999). Supplementary normalcy and otherness: Queer Asian American men reflect on stereotypes, identity, and oppression. *Qualitative Studies in Education, 12*(5), 491–508.

Kumashiro, K. (2001). *Troubling intersections of race and sexuality: Queer students of color and anti-oppressive education.* Lanham, MD: Rowman and Littlefield.

Kumashiro, K. (2002). Against repetition: Addressing resistance to anti-oppressive change in the practices of learning, teaching, supervising and researching. *Harvard Educational Review, 72*(1), 67–92.

Ladson-Billings, G. (1994). *The dreamkeepers: Successful teachers of African American students.* San Francisco: Jossey-Bass.

Ladson-Billings, G. (1995). Toward a theory of culturally relevant pedagogy. *American Educational Research Journal, 32*(3), 465–491.

Ladson-Billings, G. (2000). Racialized discourses and ethnic epistemologies. In N. K. Denzin, & Y. S. Lincoln (Eds.), *Handbook of qualitative research, second edition* (pp. 257–277). Thousand Oaks, CA: Sage Publications.

Ladson-Billings, G., & Tate, W. (1995). Toward a critical race theory of education. *Teacher's College Record, 97*(1), 47–68.

Lather, P. (1997). Drawing the line at angels: Working the ruins of feminist ethnography. *International Journal of Qualitative Studies in Education 10*(3), 285–304.

Lee, J., & M. Zhou (2004). *Asian American youth: Culture, identity and ethnicity.* New York: Routledge.

Lee, R. (1999). *Orientals: Asian Americans in popular culture.* Philadelphia, PA: Temple University Press.

Lee, S. J. (1996). *Unraveling the "model minority" stereotype: Listening to Asian American youth.* New York: Teachers College Press.

Lee, S. J. (1997). The road to college: Hmong American women's pursuit of higher education. *Harvard Educational Review, 67*(4), 803–827.

Lee, S. J. (2001). More than "model minorities" or "delinquents": A look at Hmong American high school students. *Harvard Educational Review, 71*(3), 505–528.

Lee, S. J. (2005). *Up against whiteness: Race, schools, and immigrant students.* New York: Teachers College Press.

Lei, J. (2003). (Un)necessary toughness?: Those "loud Black girls" and those "quiet Asian boys." *Anthropology and Education Quarterly, 34*(2), 158–181.

Letts, W. J., & Sears, J. T. (1999). *Queering elementary education: Advancing the dialogue about sexualities and schooling.* Lanham, MD: Rowman and Littlefield.

Lewis, O. (1969). The culture of poverty. In D. P. Moynihan (Ed.), *On understanding poverty: perspectives from the social sciences,* (pp. 187–200). New York: Basic Books.

Lincoln, S., & Guba, E. G. (1985). *Naturalistic inquiry.* Beverly Hills, CA: Sage.

Louwagie, P., & Browning, D. (2005a, October 9). Shamed into silence. *Star Tribune.* Retrieved November 15, 2006 from http://www.proquest.umi.com.

Louwagie, P., & Browning, D. (2005b, October 10). Shamed into silence: Culture clash can stymie help. *Star Tribune.* Retrieved November 15, 2006 from http://www.proquest.umi.com.

Lowe, L. (1996). *Immigrant acts: On Asian American cultural politics.* Durham, NC: Duke University Press.

Lubienski, S. T. (2003). Celebrating diversity and denying disparities: A critical assessment. *Educational Researcher, 32*(8), 30–38.

Luttrell, W. (2003). *Pregnant bodies, fertile minds: Gender, race and the schooling of pregnant teens.* New York: Routledge.

MacLure, M. (1996). Telling transitions: boundary work in narratives of becoming an action researcher. *British Education Research Journal, 22*(3), 273–286.

Maira, S. (2002). *Desis in the house: Indian American youth culture in New York City.* Philadelphia, PA: Temple University Press.

McKay, S. L., & Wong, S-L. C. (1996). Multiple discourses, multiple identities: Investment and agency in second-language learning among Chinese adolescent immigrant students. *Harvard Educational Review, 66*(3), 577–608.

McNeil, L. (2000). *Contradictions of school reform: Educational costs of standardized testing.* New York: RoutledgeFalmer.

McWhorter, J. (2000). *Losing the race: Self-sabotage in Black America.* New York: Free Press.

Michie, G. (1999). *Holler if you hear me: The education of a teacher and his students.* New York: Teachers College Press.

Miles, M. B., & Huberman, A. M. (1994). *Qualitative data analysis: A sourcebook of new methods* (2nd ed.). Thousand Oaks, CA: Sage.

Mills, S. (1997). *Discourse.* New York: Routledge.

Min, P. G. (2003). Social science research on Asian Americans. In J. A. Banks, & C. M. Banks (Eds.) *Handbook of research on multicultural education* (pp. 332–348). New York: Macmillan Publishing Company.

Mittelberg, D., & Waters, M. (1992). The process of ethnogenesis among Haitian and Israeli immigrants in the United States. *Ethnic and Racial Studies, 15*(3), 412–435.

Mohanty, C. H. (1984). Under Western eyes: Feminist scholarship and colonial discourses. *Boundary, 12*(3)-*13*(1), 333–358.

Mohanty, C. H. (1994). On race and voice: Challenges for liberal education in the 1990s. In H. Giroux, & P. McLaren (Eds.), *Between borders: Pedagogy and the politics of cultural studies* (pp. 145–166). New York: Routledge.

Moll, L., & Gonzalez, N. (2003). Engaging life: A funds of knowledge approach to multicultural education. In J. A. Banks, & C. M. Banks (Eds.) *Handbook of research on multicultural education* (pp. 699–715). New York: Macmillan Publishing Company.

Mouacheupao, K. (3 2006 February). GLBT Hmong coming out party. *Hmong Today.* Retrieved on August 6, 2008 from http://www.hmongtoday.com/displaynews.asp?ID = 2144.

Moynihan, D. P. (1965). *The negro family: The case for national action.* Washington, DC: Brookings Institute.

Ngo, B. (2002). Contesting "culture": The perspectives of Hmong American female students on early marriage. *Anthropology and Education Quarterly, 33*(2), 163–188.

Ngo, B. (2003). Citing discourses: Making sense of homophobia and hetero-normativity at Dynamic High School. *Equity and Excellence in Education, 36*(2), 115–124.

Ngo, B., & Lee, S. (2007). Complicating the image of model minority success: A review of Southeast Asian American education. *Review of Educational Research, 77*(4), 415–453.

Oakes, J. (1985). *Keeping track: How schools structure inequality.* New Haven: Yale University Press.

Omi, M., & Winant, H. (1994). *Racial formation in the United States: From the 1960s to the 1990s, second edition.* New York: Routledge.

Osajima, K. (1987). Asian Americans as the model minority: An analysis of the popular press image in the 1960s and 1980s. In G. Y. Okihiro, S. Hune, A. A. Hansen, & J. M. Lie (Eds.), *Reflections on shattered windows: Promises and prospects for Asian Americans studies* (pp. 166–174). Pullman: Washington State University Press.

Pang, V. (1990). Asian American children: A diverse population. In T. Nakanishi and T. Nishida (Eds.), *The Asian American educational experience* (pp. 167–179). New York: Routledge.

Prasso, S. (2005). *The Asian mystique: Dragon ladies, geisha girls, & our fantasies of the exotic orient.* New York: PublicAffairs.

Rainwater, L., & Yancey, W. L. (1967). *The Moynihan report and the politics of controversy: a trans-action social science and public policy report.* Cambridge, MA: MIT Press.

Reinharz, S. (1992). Feminist methods in social research. New York: Oxford University Press.

Roman, L. G. (1993). Double exposure: The politics of feminist materialist ethnography. *Educational Theory, 43*(3), 279–308.

Ross, J. D. (2007 September 7). Offended?: The rap's on me. Washington Post Retrieved on October 1, 2007 from http://www.washingtonpost.com/wp-dyn/content/article/2007/09/07/AR2007090702048.html.

Said, E. (1979). *Orientalism.* New York: Vintage Books.

Sarroub, L. K. (2005). *All American Yemeni girls: Being Muslim in a public school.* Philadelphia, PA: University of Pennsylvania Press.

Scheurich, J. (1995). A postmodern critique of research interviewing. *International Journal of Qualitative Studies in Education, 8*(3), 239–252.

Schultz, K. (2001). Constructing failure, narrating success: Rethinking the "problem" of teen pregnancy. *Teachers College Record 103*(4), 582–607.

Scott, J. (1992). Experience. In J. Butler, & J. Scott (Eds.), *Feminists theorize the political* (pp. 22–39). New York: Routledge.

Sheets, R. H. (2003). Competency vs. good intentions: Diversity ideologies and teacher potential. *International Journal of Qualitative Studies in Education, 16*(1), 111–120.

Shor, I. (1992). *Empowering education.* Chicago: University of Chicago Press.

Sleeter, C., & Stillman, J. (2005). Standardizing knowledge in a multicultural society. *Curriculum Inquiry, 35*(1), 27–46.

Stacey, J. (1988). Can there be a feminist ethnography? *Women's Studies International Forum, 11*(1), 21–27.

Stake, R. (1995). *The art of case study research.* Thousand Oaks, CA: Sage.

Strauss, A., & Corbin, J. (1998). *Basics of qualitative research: Grounded theory procedures and techniques* (2nd ed.). Newbury Park, CA: Sage.

Suarez-Orozco, M. (2001). Globalization, immigration and education: The research agenda. *Harvard Educational Review, 71*(1), 345–365.

Takaki, R. (1989). *Strangers from a different shore: A history of Asian Americans.* New York: Penguin Books.

Tapia, J. (1998). The schooling of Puerto Ricans: Philadelphia's most impoverished community. *Anthropology and Education Quarterly 29(3)*, 297–323.

Taylor, C. (1994). The politics of recognition. In D. T. Goldberg (Ed.), *Multiculturalism: A Critical Reader* (pp. 75–105). Malden, Massachusetts: Blackwell Publishers, Inc.

Taylor, K. H. (1998 March 22). Somalis in America: Working through a clash of cultures. *Start Tribune*, 1A.

Tillotson, K. (1994 April 21). The comeback kids. *Star Tribune*, 1E.

Toch, T., Gest, T., & Guttman, M. (1993 November 8). Violence in schools. *US News and World Report*. Retrieved June 6, 2008 from http://www.usnews.com/usnews/news/articles/931108/archive_016059_5.htm.

Toppo, G. (2006 June 20). Big city schools struggle with graduation rates. *USA Today*. Retrieved June 6, 2008 http://www.usatoday.com/news/education/2006-06-20-dropout-rates_x.htm.

Trinh, T. M-H. (1986/1987). Introduction, *Discourse*, 8, 3–9.

Trinh, T. M-H. (1991). *When the moon waxes red: Representation, gender and cultural politics*. New York: Routledge.

Tuan, M. (1998). *Forever foreigners or honorary whites?* New Burnswick: Rutgers University Press.

Valenzuela, A. (1999). *Subtractive schooling: U.S. Mexican youth and the politics of caring*. Albany, NY: State University of New York Press.

Van Maanen, J. (1988). *Tales of the field: On writing ethnography*. Chicago: University of Chicago Press.

Watkins, S. C. (2006). *Hip hop matters: Politics, pop culture, and the struggle for the soul of a movement*. Boston, MA: Beacon Press.

Wax, E. (1998). Mother's fray: Culture clash puts special strain on immigrant moms and daughters. *Newsday*, May 10. Retrieved November 15, 2006 from http://www.proquest.umi.com.

West, T. R. (2002). *Signs of struggle: The rhetorical politics of cultural difference*. New York: SUNY Press.

Weedon, C. (1987). *Feminist practice and poststructuralist theory*. New York: Basil Blackwell.

Wilson, W. J. (1987). *The truly disadvantaged: The inner city, the underclass and public policy*. Chicago, IL: University of Chicago Press.

Wilson, W. J. (1991). The truly disadvantaged revisited: A response to Hochschild and Boxill. *Ethics, 101(3)*, 593–609.

Wolcott, H. F. (1994). *Transforming qualitative data: Description, analysis, and interpretation*. Thousand Oaks, CA: Sage.

Wolf, M. (1992). *A thrice-told tale: Feminism, postmodernism and ethnographic responsibility*. Palo Alto, CA: Stanford University Press.

Yon, D. (2000). *Elusive culture: Schooling, race and identity in global times*. New York: State University of New York Press.

Zhou, M., & Bankston, C. L. (1998). *Growing up American: How Vietnamese children adapt to life in the United States*. New York, NY: Russell Sage Foundation.

Zhou, M., & Kim, S. (2006). Community forces, social capital, and educational achievement: The case of supplementary education in the Chinese and Korean immigrant communities. *Harvard Educational Review, 76(1)*, 1–29.

Index

naturalizing, 10
referring to discourses, 53
of teachers and staff, 44, 49, 99, 103
diversity, 31, 34, 37, 63, 77, 130n6
celebrating, 37–38, 103
of cultures, 34
as difference, 104
of groups, 55
real, 37
of students, 30, 31
See also multicultural education and multiculturalism
dominant discourses, 3, 33–34, 85, 106, 109–110
as binary oppositions, 2, 5
defined, 10
failures of, 2
as ingrained, 10
as natural, 10
double movement. See identity: double movement of
drugs, 3, 4, 23, 92, 118
Dynamic High School, 29–30
background, 124–125, 130n4
diversity, 30–31, 37, 130–131n6
neighborhood, 29
past, 23, 26:
gang violence, 25
low attendance, 25
low standards, 24
students, 29:
comeback kids, 50–51
immigrants, 40–41
poverty of, 30, 39, 50, 130n5
resilience of, 50
transformation, 27–28:
leadership in, 27
process of, 27, 28

easy stories, 5, 18, 51, 52
ethnic identity, 57–59
ethnography
crisis of representation, x
as dynamic, x
as irony, ix

opportunity for exploitation, 113
as partial, 16
personal connections, 113, 121
poststructuralist, 9, 16, 129n2
process of, 14–15
as telling stories, 19, 20
See also poststructuralist ethnography; telling stories; writing ethnography

Fine, Michelle, 51–52
Foucault, Michel, 9
Freedom Writers, 3

gangs, 3, 5, 50, 88–90, 92–93, 95, 109
gangster, 1, 76, 96
gangster-fronting behavior, 75, 77, 80, 86, 96, 100, 105, 106
gay
students, 15, 106, 113
harassment, 76–77, 100, 113–115, 129n5. See also homophobia
geisha girls, 61
good/bad, 5, 7, 21, 80, 98, 103–104
good student, 80, 82, 88, 90, 96. See also bad student
Gilroy, Paul, 32, 53

Hmong Club, 62, 63, 67
home life, 30, 40–44
homeplace, 48
homophobia, 78, 100–101, 113, 114–115
honor roll, 18, 79, 96, 132n2
hooks, bell, 48, 107
hybridity, 6, 12, 73. See also Bhabha, Homi

identity, 8, 9, 10–11, 65, 69–70, 98, 105–107
ambivalence (see ambivalence of identity)
contradictions of, 98
creating space for negotiation, 12, 65, 73, 76
defined, 10–11